DESIGNER

# FURNITURE
## Anyone Can Make

WILLIAM E. SCHREMP

 Simon and Schuster □ New York

Copyright © 1972 by William E. Schremp
All rights reserved
including the right of reproduction
in whole or in part in any form
Published by Simon and Schuster
Rockefeller Center, 630 Fifth Avenue
New York, New York 10020

First printing
SBN 671-21283-4
Library of Congress Catalog Card Number: 72-83906
Designed by Beri Greenwald
Manufactured in the United States of America
Printed by The Murray Printing Company, Forge Village, Mass.
Bound by The Book Press, Brattleboro, Vt.

To Gerry, who, as I suppose all writers' wives must,
looked at draft after draft
until she is something of an authority herself.

And to Frank, who, although he wasn't aware of it
at the time, was largely responsible
for the existence of this book.

# Contents

# Preface

This is a different sort of do-it-yourself book in a number of ways. Perhaps most important, it is aimed at today's people, who not only need activity or the satisfaction of creating something with their hands; they need furniture! It will guide them through the steps of building pieces for every room of the house. Indeed, using these methods and materials, they can build virtually all the furniture in their home.

It also introduces the reader to some of today's materials and techniques. There is nothing here about how to apply a satisfactory wet finish to unfinished furniture (you can't, really) or how to brighten door panels with gaily colored adhesive paper. The pieces built from these designs will be around — and looking like new — as long as the builders are.

The reader is not directed to build a sofa or bed as I happened to like it or need it but is advised to modify the designs to his own likes or needs. He can combine this basic shape with that detail, build to the appropriate size, and have a truly custom piece of furniture — at lumberyard prices.

Although some of the materials and methods may be unfamiliar, there is nothing in the book beyond the capabilities of the most inexperienced builder. Each piece is broken down into basic steps, none of them more complicated than thousands of things he does every day.

I've tried to avoid sounding like a technical manual. The book is written with my years of trial and error — some magnificent — close at hand. My hope is that with some of my mistakes as examples, the reader will be able to avoid them. Perhaps he will invent some of his own, but that's called experience.

Tucking into one small book designs and instructions for a houseful of furniture, plus introductions to materials and techniques perhaps new to the reader, required a new approach. The chapters on materials and methods apply to all the designs and must be read carefully. The methods proceed through the construction of a small cube table or similar simple piece. Focusing on the cube is admittedly a literary device, but more than that, it's a very low-cost and quickly completed piece for the reader to make all the mistakes on. Don't just read about it; build it! The cube is compatible with whatever else will be built from this book.

To make so many designs possible, there are complete instructions for only the most basic pieces. Then, alternative or additional techniques for building the variations are described as they apply. To build the last sofa, you must read about the first one first.

I hope you won't find that such a chore.

W.E.S.

Huntington, New York
April 1972

# DESIGNER FURNITURE
## Anyone Can Make

# Chapter One

# INTRODUCTION

Throughout the country—indeed, throughout the world—countless homes and museums display treasured do-it-yourself projects, mementos of the days when you did it yourself or did without. The earliest settlers in America had to produce with their own hands the tools, homes, furniture, and other wares that they needed for survival. These early craftsmen were, for the most part, untrained in their art, but some developed remarkable skills. And, of course, these men and their successors became the suppliers to the rest of the community.

Part of the American's nature is to build things for himself, whether from need or from whim. The preschooler is given a Playskool workbench with toy tools; when he reaches grade school his room is crowded with model airplanes or plastic cars or radio kits. When he reaches high school he is trying to redesign a 1953 Chevy. The pattern holds in later years. Per capita sales of hand and power tools in the United States far exceed those of Europe.

But this great do-it-yourself energy hasn't always been manifest in home furnishings. Over the centuries since the Jamestown settlement, homemade furniture was still largely the result of critical need: as late as 1912, Americans were still homesteading, carrying all their belongings into the wilderness in a single wagon. There were exceptions, of course. There have always been a few gifted amateurs with a command over that most common and difficult of construction materials—wood.

After the industrial revolution it wasn't unheard of, but it was rare, to find a young man who would undertake from choice to furnish his first home with his own hands. Finally home from long hours of work, he just didn't have much time for such things; materials and hardware weren't always readily available; hand tools were both scarce and crude; and power tools were unknown. And he probably didn't think of it anyway; it wasn't "the thing to do."

Somewhere around the end of World War II all this changed. Partly because of the time necessary for a furniture industry to convert from the production of war materials, but mostly because of a lack of ready cash shared by millions of young men thrust back into a newly peacetime economy, an important cultural change occurred in America. You may remember it, with varying degrees of fondness, as the decorate-your-own-home-with-painted-orange-crates era.

Early postwar low-cost decorating was a marvel of innovation and in its own way as significant as earlier, more-formal furniture periods. Prior to the age of the orange crate, salvaged pieces, unlikely materials, and found objects had been used to provide furnishings for one's home, but this time it was different. This time, if the owners displayed even a touch of humor, it was socially O.K.

It's hard to imagine returning Civil War veterans, who also suffered from a lack of money and materials, showing off to each other the clever book storage they had created from bricks and old boards, but it was indeed a source of pride and fun for ex-GIs and their families. An honest-to-Pete 1947 painted orange crate belongs in the collection of the Museum of Modern Art, because that inexpensive — free! — and functional piece marks the point when young Americans began to influence directly and share in the creation of their own environment.

Much that was discovered then lives on — indeed prevails — today. Lacking chinoiserie vases or French tole, postwar housewives planted their house plants in clay pots, the same clay pots that show up today in *House and Garden* as well as *Progressive Architecture*. Lamps were wildly expensive to youngsters furnishing their first apartment, and pretty much out of place in a Quonset hut anyway, so they were replaced by such devices as Oriental paper lanterns hung over a bare bulb, styling not unlike much of today's architectural and residential lighting. Often lacking the sofa and chairs they were used to in their parents' home, young couples happily sat on pillows or hassocks and served coffee or drinks in jelly glasses. Lacking a proper bedstead, they put the mattress on the floor, and later on six little screw-in legs, a device that set the tone for much of today's bedroom design.

Most young couples didn't realize it at the time, but they were really discovering, and providing an enthusiastic market for, design concepts of a remarkable group of young designers suddenly thrust into national prominence. Such new-thinkers as George Nelson, Charles Eames, Eero Saarinen, Paul McCobb, and Milo Baughman visualized home furnishings in ways that would have seemed quite odd to most earlier designers, but Nelson's then wildly innovative wall systems, for example, surely didn't seem odd to a couple who had tried to accomplish essentially the same thing with orange crates, bricks, and boards.

These men, along with some later designers, are largely responsible for what we today call "contemporary" furniture. And in creating these new shapes and forms, devising new manufacturing techniques, they created a furniture period with a quality shared by no earlier period: styling that lends itself to the home workshop.

Duplication of most furniture of the past calls for talents far beyond those of most amateurs. The intricate carvings on many traditional pieces are themselves works of art. The necessary strength in legs and frames calls for the use of woods and joining methods that pretty much defeat most home tools and techniques. The professional upholsterer is a highly trained craftsman.

Probably the single biggest problem for the amateur furniture-maker is the finish. The lovely wood finish on an expensive dining table is not simply the result of a quart of varnish and a lot of loving sanding and rubbing. It is achieved with high-speed finishing machines, air-controlled spray booths, coatings not generally available to or usable by the retail customer, and drying ovens. The result is pretty hard to simulate in the basement on a Saturday afternoon.

The pieces in this book call for none of these facilities or techniques. Like their commercial equivalents, they are largely constructed of plywood, in most cases assembled with nails, and require a level of craftsmanship well within the reach of most amateurs. Instead of paint or other wet finishes, most of these pieces are finished with plastic laminate, a material that (regardless of what you've always supposed) is quite easy to work with and eliminates any "homemade" look.

The seating pieces are "upholstered" with foam mattresses or cushions—with zippered covers well within the capabilities of the home dressmaker or inexpensive to order from your local seamstress. Some case pieces include drawers and doors, but if you want to eliminate these more tricky aspects of furniture building, there are alternative approaches.

You can build almost everything in the book without expensive tools. Many people use a belt sander and a router when working with plastic laminate, but you can achieve the same result—a little more slowly—with about $15 worth of specialized hand tools made for the professional cabinet installer. A table saw is a little faster for cutting plywood, but the finished piece will look just as good if you cut it in your kitchen with a saber saw —or with an old-fashioned handsaw, for that matter.

Some of the designs will call for specialized hardware or suggest devices that you may not have seen in your local hardware store. Check the Buyer's Guide at the back of the book for mail sources of items not widely distributed. Your dealer will be able to order most of the items from his normal sources of supply. Such special orders generally take a week or so.

You'll need a hammer, of course, and a screwdriver and sandpaper, but what you need most is confidence. None of these pieces calls for more than sawing a reasonably straight line, driving a nail straight, and reading carefully.

It's not intended, of course, that every reader will want to build these pieces himself. Most local craftsmen are familiar with the techniques and materials and if not, like you, can produce quality pieces by following the directions.

Neither is it intended that everything should be built exactly as it is shown. If you really need a sofa only $24\frac{1}{4}$ inches high to fit properly under a window, by all means make it that high. If your family tends to be a bit tall or a bit short, you can produce a custom dining table that fits you all more comfortably. By picking a design here and an idea there, you can produce a custom piece that exactly serves your needs, a luxury you rarely find in ready-made furniture.

# Chapter Two

---

# THE MATERIALS

Although some alternative materials will be suggested from time to time, virtually all the designs employ one or more of four basic materials—plywood and related boards, plastic laminates, Plexiglas, and a system of extruded aluminum shapes and castings.

## PLYWOOD AND RELATED BOARDS

There is evidence that plywood, in one form or another, has been used since the earliest days of civilization. But, although apparently they haven't thought to claim its invention, the Russians introduced the commercial production of plywood in the 1880s.

Among the many virtues of plywood for furniture building are its availability in relatively large sheets, its strength in all directions, and the fact that its cross-grained layers counteract the natural inclination of wood to warp.

There are two basic types of plywood, interior and exterior, the distinction being in whether or not the glue that holds the layers together is waterproof. Interior plywood is appropriate for most pieces of furniture and is not damaged by occasional spillage or high humidity. For kitchen or bathroom countertops, vanity cabinets, wet bars, and similar items where there may be some doubt, specify exterior grade. Interior-grade plywood is generally available in thicknesses of $\frac{1}{4}''$, $\frac{3}{8}''$, $\frac{1}{2}''$, $\frac{5}{8}''$, and $\frac{3}{4}''$. Exterior-grade material is made in the same thicknesses, with the exception of $\frac{5}{16}''$ instead of $\frac{1}{4}''$.

When you order plywood your dealer is likely to ask what grade you need, and use such terms as A-A, A-D, and B-D. The letters refer to the quality of the two plywood faces, and the A's cost a good deal more than the D's, so don't buy better quality than you need. (Although some manufacturers obviously make better-quality products than others, these grade designations have nothing to do with quality as such.)

N and A are the highest grades of face veneer and add nothing to the quality of a finished piece unless it is to be painted. B-grade faces, which contain a number of "boat patches"* but have a smooth surface, are ideal for lamination.

---

* Because fir, the board most commonly used for plywood, is so full of knots, almost any sheet of A- or B-grade material will require some repair work on its surface. The knot is removed from the sheet of veneer as you would use a cookie cutter; then the space is filled with a similarly shaped plug.

C grade means that the face can have a number of "tight knots," that is, knots that haven't fallen out and still provide a smooth surface. D means that the knots have fallen out, leaving voids or holes.

An empty knothole an inch or so across is all right under a surface of plastic laminate unless it falls at an edge (see Figure 1), leaving the plastic unsupported at that point. Use D grade with perfect confidence, but be sure that your saw cuts don't leave a void at an edge. The same is true of C, because those "tight knots" generally prove to be not so tight when you saw through them.

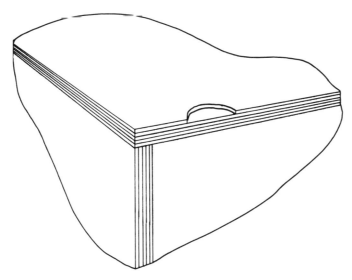

Figure 1. A void falling at an edge doesn't provide adequate support for plastic laminate. The same knothole away from the edge causes no problems at all.

Particle board is another sheet material used for commercial laminated furniture production, and it often has the virtue of being a little less expensive than plywood. But it also has some offsetting disadvantages: it's heavier than plywood, it tends to be more brittle and harder to work with, and screws pull out of it quite easily. Use it only if none of these matters, which is unlikely.

Hardboard is not appropriate for basic construction, but you will find occasional use for thin sheets in forming curved surfaces. In some cases it can be used for cabinet backs.

## PLASTIC LAMINATES

High-pressure plastic laminates have long been a familiar part of the American home: covering the kitchen countertops of more than a generation, serving as tops for bathroom vanities, breakfast tables, home bars and such, even showing up once in a while on a coffee table. But, by and large, laminates were long considered utility materials, not to be brought out for company.

All this has changed quite drastically. Furniture finished with laminates exists commercially for every room in the house, and the laminate is produced in a wide spectrum of colors, textures, patterns, and specialized designs. But although welcome today throughout the house, laminates are only now being welcomed into a few home workshops.

The home craftsman hasn't taken proper advantage of this valuable material for two reasons: First, kitchen counters are quite expensive when done by most cabinet shops. If it's that expensive, he reasoned, there must be something terribly complicated about working with the material. This is not true, of course, but there was no one to tell him so.

And that's the second reason. Of the many producers of plastic laminate, none to date has chosen to expend any significant effort in the do-it-yourself market to educate the buyer. The reasoning is simple: Until recently the producers couldn't see any real return for such efforts. (After all, how many kitchen countertops could the amateur make?) This is not true now; there's a substantial potential home market, and you'll be seeing more and more consumer-oriented information from the producers.

The simple virtue of laminate as a material for amateurs is that it is already factory-finished and the finish will remain fresh and bright throughout all your fabricating steps and for many years hence. Because it is rigid and has a degree of structural integrity, it can cover a multitude of sins on a plywood substructure. Any other finish — paint, varnish, even vinyl sheeting and vinyl fabrics — necessitates filling nail holes and the pores of the wood and sanding the grain smooth. After all that, if you've produced a really satisfactory finish, you're something of an artist yourself.

Not so with plastic laminates. Knots, hammer dents, grain, bad saw-cuts — all disappear under the stiff plastic. As long as the surface is flush and the corners sharp, your carpentry is just fine.

A complete line of laminate colors and textures may comprise a hundred or so separate items. Double that number, because each may be available in either satin or low-glare finish, and you have quite a range of products to choose from. Your dealer can obtain whatever you need from his distributor in a couple of days. Don't be trapped by impatience and buy whatever you happen to find in his stock. If you can wait, you'll be able to choose from a range of lovely colors as well as such specialties as good wood grains, a slate that looks and *feels* like the real thing, and cane, with real cane encapsulated in the plastic sheet.

Laminate will cost, depending on the brand, locality, and pricing policy of the dealer, between 40 and 90 cents per square foot. In some cases you will be able to buy just the amount you need; in others, particularly when you special-order, you will have to buy complete 4' × 8' sheets. (Sheets 4' × 10' and 4' × 12' are sometimes available on special order but fetch a premium price.) If your particular effort will leave a good deal of scrap, plan to build something smaller along with the larger piece. Because of the techniques involved, two simultaneous projects often take little more time than a single one.

## PLEXIGLAS

Plexiglas, like plastic laminate, has been around for quite a while, but unlike the kitchen-oriented laminate, it has indeed been in the parlor. In your mind's eye, perhaps you can see the likes of Jean Harlow or Joan Crawford reclining on a chaise longue of white fur and clear plastic, curved and shaped in fanciful ways. Clear plastic furniture was considered quite classy in the thirties but like many other movie totems of the era—Duesenbergs, Long Island estates, and white grand pianos—didn't much influence the mass market.

Today Plexiglas is an important material in home furnishings design.* It is gaining commercial popularity in all manner of furniture, from small occasional tables, clock cases, and the like, to sofas, molded chairs, and other larger pieces.

A few hobbyists have always worked in acrylic plastic, but until a manufacturer decided to put some special effort into educating the home craftsman market, the material, like plastic laminate, suffered because it looked, somehow, hard to deal with. Remembering that you've always been pretty sloppy with glue, how could you ever hope to achieve one of those perfectly clear joints, seemingly melded by the hands of an angel, or at least a master craftsman? The truth is, the nature of the material and the adhesive pretty much take care of the problem for you. In fact, if you follow the directions carefully, you'll really have to make a special effort to goof up a joint.

Some of the designs to follow use Plexiglas as a material to fabricate into furniture; others use it simply as a sheet for such applications as sliding doors or protective tabletops.

Plexiglas is sold through lumber dealers, hardware stores, paint and wallpaper stores, hobby shops, and any number of other outlets. Like the laminates, it comes in a range of sheet sizes, colors, clear, translucent, opaque, bronze, smoke, as well as various thicknesses and textures, so your dealer may not have what you want in stock. He too can special-order for you and have your material in a few days. He will also stock such special tools as an inexpensive cutter to eliminate sawing, a strip heater for making simple bends in the material, and a needle applicator for the adhesive.

Quarter-inch Plexiglas costs approximately $2.50 per square foot, proportionally more or less for other thicknesses. If a conventional dealer isn't handy, you can likely

---

* Although Plexiglas is a trademark of the Rohm & Haas company for its brand of acrylic plastic sheet, I'll use the term more or less generically because the material is widely marketed under that name, because no other manufacturer is currently making either the material or the few special tools widely available to the home market, and because if you asked most lumber dealers for acrylic sheet, you'd likely get either a blank stare or a polystyrene sheet, which isn't the same thing at all.

buy the material from a plastics distributor, often at reduced cost. Look in your Yellow Pages.

Although most distributors stock thicknesses over $\frac{1}{4}''$, the heavier material cannot be easily cut with home equipment. (A carbide-tipped saw blade is required, and it costs a good deal more than conventional saw blades.) If you want to use the heavier material, most distributors are equipped to cut it to a specified size. The other steps—drilling, polishing, and such, but not bending—can be accomplished at home with no further difficulty.

## ALUMINUM SHAPES AND CASTINGS

The aluminum components used throughout this book add a new range and flexibility to the home construction of furniture. They serve the same purpose that the exquisitely fabricated and polished stainless steel serves on higher-style and higher-priced commercial pieces. But unlike the welded stainless, an aluminum system is assembled very much like a Tinker Toy: cast corners fit into sections of square aluminum tubing, locking together to form the structure. The metal can be sanded or wire-brushed to achieve a satin finish, or it can be polished with home equipment. If you choose, you can take the completed assembly to a local plating firm to have it chromed.

Because of the wide range of castings and extruded shapes in the aluminum system, dealer stocking is difficult. The system can be ordered directly from the manufacturer, with the tubing cut to your specifications without charge. (See listing in Buyer's Guide.)

# Chapter Three

# THE METHODS

## THE CUBE

Certainly the best way to learn to do anything is to do it, so we'll begin by building a simple cube table that will illustrate most of the principles of plastic lamination. And the cube, simply a plywood box (see Figure 2), forms the basis of most of the designs to follow.

First, what plywood to use? As a general rule, $\frac{3}{4}''$ material is best for all furniture construction. It's stiff enough to resist flexing or sagging when spanning long dimensions, and it provides adequate nail strength when nails enter its edge. Also, it has the proper scale and "look" for the type of furniture in this book. For specific components,

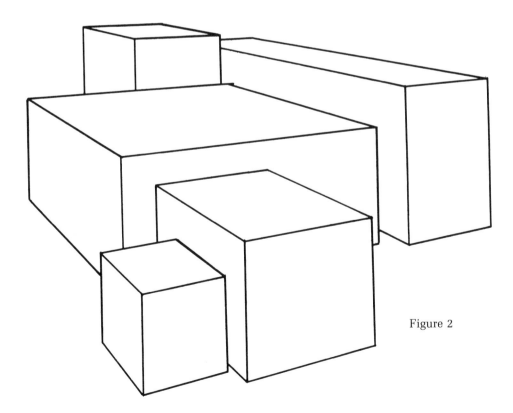

Figure 2

such as some sofa shells, lighter plywood will be suggested to save weight and a little money. But use the lighter material *only* where nails entering its edge don't carry the major structural burden—that is to say, where you might split the plywood when you sit on it!

Begin each project, even the simplest, by making a sketch (see Figure 3). It needn't look like much, but it will enable you to keep track of all your dimensions. Often, on a more complex piece, if you try to carry all the specifications in your head, you will forget to add or subtract the thickness of one component or another—all of which add up to your final over-all dimension—and will thus cut pieces too long or too short. And the sketch is further important because many of the designs are meant to be built to *your* dimensions, not to the arbitrary lengths and heights specified here.

This will be a 16″ cube, although you can work right along with any other size that strikes your fancy. (When I speak here of a 16″ cube or later of an 84″ sofa or whatever, I'm speaking of the dimensions of the plywood structure. In fact, the finished cube will be 16″ *plus* the thickness of the plastic applied to it. Unless you have some special problems, or a particularly clear grasp of arithmetic, don't get yourself all snarled up trying to produce a piece that's 16″ or whatever *including* the plastic.)

Most commercially produced cigarette or snack tables are between 15″ and 16″ high and, of course, vary widely in the other dimensions. Cocktail or coffee tables are also generally 16″ or so high, typically 60″ long and between 20″ and 30″ wide—your choice depends on your space. Lamp or end tables are typically 14″ or so wide but should relate to the depth and arm height of the sofa or chair they accompany.

Using $\frac{3}{4}$″ plywood, cut the top of the cube 16″ × 16″. The sides, because they sit under the top, are 16″ wide but only $15\frac{1}{4}$″ high. The ends, which sit under the top and

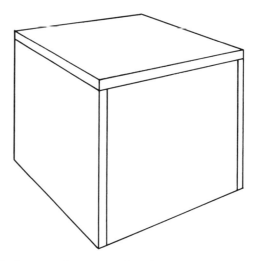

Figure 3. *A simple sketch will help you dope out the dimensions of each of your components.*

between the two $\frac{3}{4}''$ sides, are $15\frac{1}{4}''$ high and $14\frac{1}{2}''$ wide. This all may sound pretty obvious, but you'd be surprised how many experienced builders — including the writer — have forgotten to account for one dimension or the other and have had to recut a project.

Assemble the cube with sixpenny (2″) finishing nails every 6 inches or so and drive the heads flush with the wood surface. Try to avoid hammer dents if possible. If the plywood you use has one C or D face, that is, with knots, keep that face to the inside. It's not often critical, but learn the habit of keeping the best face outward.

Although laminates do indeed cover all manner of construction sins, the job is easier if the plywood structure is built of properly sized components with accurate and smooth saw cuts. Rule number one is to have a sharp saw blade. Dull blades tend to chew at the wood, leaving rough edges that require more than the usual sanding and make plastic-trimming operations more difficult.

A number of different blade-types are available. If you're using a table or radial-arm saw, a veneer blade, although a bit more expensive, is best for precision cutting of plywood. A "ply tooth" blade will provide accurate cuts, but if one isn't available at the moment, a sharp all-purpose blade will do.

With a hand saber or jig saw, use a medium-tooth plywood blade.

In cutting with a table or radial-arm saw, accuracy is no trick at all, but if you're using any kind of hand-held power saw, don't try to follow a line freehand. Clamp a straightedge on the work to guide the cut. Whatever saw you use, be sure that the blade is set perfectly vertical, producing an accurate 90° angle.

If you'd rather not do the sawing yourself, lumber dealers will generally provide cut-to-your-specifications plywood for a slight additional cost. Don't, however, drop in on a busy Saturday afternoon and expect to get the job done in a few minutes. Try to catch your dealer on a slow day during the week so you can talk over the project and give him a day or so to complete the cutting. Most dealers are surprisingly helpful when they're not rushed, and understandably unhelpful when eight other customers are waiting.

An accurately cut and carefully assembled structure requires little sanding. Just be sure all the splinters are taken off, and eliminate any bumps or ridges in the wood that would prevent the stiff plastic from lying perfectly flat.

## LAMINATING SEQUENCES

Although a cube is the same in all dimensions, it has three different *kinds* of sides or surfaces. Surface A is the top, which includes within its boundaries no rough plywood edges. The B surfaces are the sides, which include only the rough edge of the top. The C surfaces are the ends, which include both the edge of the top and the edge of the sides. (See Figure 4.)

The identity of these three distinctive surfaces is important because the plastic laminate must be applied to the table or any other piece in the proper sequence. The reason: Each piece of plastic is cut and applied a bit oversize, then trimmed flush before the succeeding piece is applied. The trimming is accomplished by making a pass along the edge of the plastic with a router or laminate trimmer. It is guided by the adjacent surface, much as the flanged wheel of a railroad car is guided along the rail. If the adjacent surface is smooth, the cut will be smooth. If the surface is not smooth, like the sawn edge of plywood, then the cut will reproduce exactly the rough shape. (Think of the machine that makes you a new house key by copying the tooth pattern of your old one.)

A proper application sequence minimizes guiding on an edge. By applying the plastic first to the two C surfaces, trimming them, then to the B surfaces, then to the top (see Figure 4), you have made all your trims while encountering a plywood edge only when trimming the C surfaces. Since these edges are later covered by the plastic on the B surfaces, any small irregularity is unimportant.

When building one or the other of the designs to follow, you may find that the A surface is not necessarily the top, but it will be there somewhere. Following the sequence will assure you a better finishing job.

## PRELIMINARY CUTTING OF THE LAMINATE

Plastic laminate can be cut to the rough size with almost any kind of saw or with a laminate scoring tool. (See Buyer's Guide.) When using a saw, remember that the teeth must cut *into* the decorative *face* of the plastic, not into the back. With a saber saw or a 7″ saw (often called a "builder's" saw), cut with the decorative face down. Using a table saw or handsaw calls for the face up. If the teeth cut into the back, they are likely to chip away some of the decorative face on the way out, often spoiling the piece of plastic.

The laminate is nearly indestructible when bonded to a surface, but an unsupported sheet is brittle, so try not to wave it around a lot. Keep the sheet well supported on a flat surface when cutting it, particularly when handling a full 4′ × 8′.

Because of the brittleness of the laminate, a scoring cutter, which looks a bit like a linoleum knife, is often best for cutting laminate. Lay the sheet on a flat surface, colored side up, and run the cutter along a straightedge. Don't press too hard; if you cut gently, the blade will stay in its track nicely. Score over and over until you have cut through the colored layer—perhaps five or six strokes. Break upward toward the colored face. If the laminate doesn't break easily, score again a couple of times and it will snap off with a nice clean break.

If you are experienced in working with laminate, a $\frac{1}{4}$″ margin on each edge is sufficient. If you are a beginner with plastic, give yourself $\frac{1}{2}$″ or so. You may need the greater margin because the adhesive sticks tight the instant the plastic touches the plywood. The greater margin will give you a little more leeway for error when you lay the plastic on the wood.

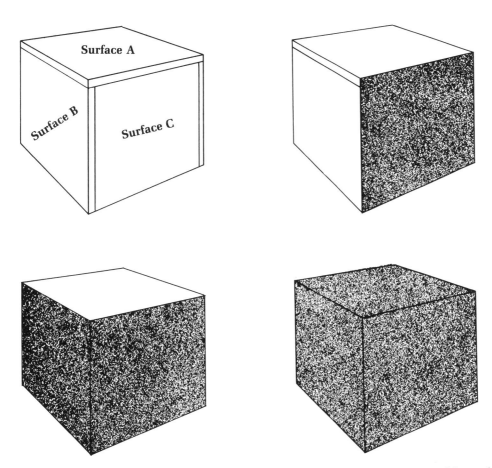

Figure 4. *A proper laminating sequence covers rough edges as early as possible in the sequence.*

## THE ADHESIVE

Plastic laminate is applied with contact adhesive, something like a heavy-duty version of the rubber cement you used in school. Contact is safe when used properly but, like many household products, can be hazardous if used improperly. It's flammable and should not be used around an open flame, cigarettes, pipes, and such. If you're working in the basement, you might even shut off the furnace while the adhesive can is open. The fumes can also get to you, so be sure that your work space is ventilated. In good weather, the backyard is a dandy place for laminating.

Contact adhesive is applied both to the back of the plastic and to the plywood surface. You can use a roller, a serrated scraper blade, or a small brush, but a cheap throw-away brush is probably handiest. Try not to leave any loose bristles in the adhesive.

Apply the adhesive in a smooth, even coating, avoiding any puddles or heavy spots, which would be slower in drying. Apply it to the plastic first, then the wood surface. Adhesive tends to dry a little faster on wood than on plastic because wood absorbs some of the solvent, so applying the adhesive to the plastic first should make both surfaces ready for use about the same time.

Let both surfaces dry to the touch—this should take twenty or thirty minutes. When the surfaces appear dull and have lost their tackiness, you are ready to begin laminating.

(Because of this drying delay, many craftsmen build two pieces at the same time, working on one while the other is drying. Because this can reduce material waste as well as save time, it is a worthwhile scheme. But be sure to keep your drying surfaces away from other operations. Sawdust in the air or flying chips from a trimming operation can create quite a mess in the wet adhesive.)

If you apply the plastic to the plywood while there are still spots, however small, of wet adhesive, the solvent vapors released by the still-drying adhesive will be trapped and may well raise a bubble in the surface. (If such bubbles do occur, they can generally be eliminated later with a hot iron.)

Try to apply the plastic as soon as possible after the adhesive is ready. A couple of hours' delay won't create any problems, but you shouldn't leave the job overnight, because the adhesive will begin curing and loose some of its bonding strength. It can also accumulate dust from the air. If you must leave it overnight, apply another light coat in the morning before continuing your work.

You're likely to find some difficulty working with contact cement in temperatures below 65° F, and the plastic also gets pretty brittle. When it's too cool, you may find that the adhesive won't bond properly and you'll run into such infuriating problems as the lifting of corners and edges.

If it is absolutely necessary to laminate in temperatures below 65°, use two coats of adhesive on each surface—let the first one dry before applying the second one —and try to bring the plastic sheets into a warmer room three or four hours before use so that they will not be too brittle when you apply them to the work. Any lifting of the plastic can be corrected by literally ironing the plastic down with a medium-hot iron. Because the thermostats of irons aren't always dependable, test the heat on a piece of scrap before applying the iron to your work. Too much heat can scorch or blister the surface.

After your piece is complete, remove whatever adhesive drippings or smears you can as soon as possible. Most can be peeled or rolled off. Although the adhesive is dry to the touch, it gets progressively harder to remove because it continues curing and hardening for quite a while. Leave the adhesive you can't peel off for later removal with a solvent. If you use a solvent immediately, some of it may "wick" in under the plastic, softening the still uncured coating. Wait a couple of days for solvent cleaning if you can, or at least use it sparingly and carefully. Ask your dealer for the proper solvent for your adhesive. Solvents like lacquer thinner do not really work properly.

## APPLYING PLASTIC TO PLYWOOD

Bringing together the plastic and the plywood is a critical step, so follow the proper techniques carefully for a foolproof lamination. The trick is simply to lay it down in the right place the first time, because contact adhesive won't permit moving the plastic around. (It's often stated that once the plastic has been brought into contact with the work, you can't get it up again. This is not strictly true. Although you can't move it around, you can get it *up* again but not without a whale of a lot of mess and trouble.)

Small pieces of plastic are applied by gripping them in both hands, up around the second joint of the fingers, leaving the fingertips free to feel the target and guide the plastic down properly. If the plastic sheet is too large for you to control easily, ask for help or use the techniques described below for larger sheets.

As soon as you see that you have placed the plastic improperly, stop all movement. At this point, chances are that all the plastic hasn't made contact, so don't let it go any further if you can avoid it. Yelling for your spouse will help. Hold the surfaces apart where you can with scraps of wood or plastic or anything else you can reach. Then begin peeling the plastic carefully away from the wood. Get your fingers under the sheet as close to the point of contact as possible, and pry it up gingerly (remember that the sheet is relatively brittle). Chances are that you can get it off in one piece.

Both surfaces will be a mess, with the adhesive peeled off some spots and piled up on others. Remove any large accumulations and start all over again. You're not likely to forget the lesson.

When applying larger pieces of plastic like a full dining-table top or sofa back, use battens to keep the surfaces apart (see Figure 5). Lay wood strips like railroad ties

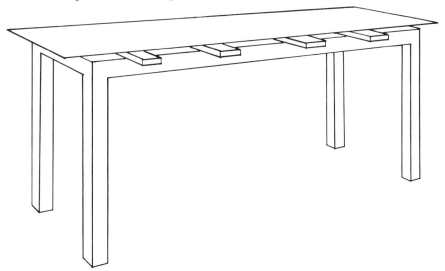

Figure 5. *Battens help you avoid disaster when applying large sheets of plastic.*

every 10″ or 12″ along the full length of your work. Lay the plastic sheet on the battens directly above its intended location but held from contact by the battens. Check the alignment all the way around. Then carefully remove the first batten and join the surfaces lightly. Check again, then remove the remaining battens one by one until the surfaces are completely joined.

Complete the bond by tapping the whole surface with a hammer on a scrap of wood to protect the surface, or use a plastic- or leather-faced hammer. Professionals secure the bond with steel rollers, but your hammer will be adequate. Be sure to concentrate on edges and corners, where lifting of the plastic is most likely.

## TRIMMING THE LAMINATE

The trimming stage is the most important in fabrication of laminated furniture because proper trimming is what gives your finished piece the machined, quality look of commercial furniture. This stage calls for both edge-sanding and machine-trimming of the laminate. The sanding can be accomplished with either a belt sander — quickest and most efficient — or an orbital or vibrating sander, slower but otherwise fine.

## THE ROUTER

Routers, the most commonly used power tools for laminate work, are priced at $30 up. Although better-quality power tools are always the best investment, low-cost routers are entirely adequate for laminate work because such work doesn't put any great strain on the machine and you're using it only for short periods of time.

There are two types of cutting bits for the router — the straight cutter and the bevel cutter. The first makes an almost-flush 90° cut, leaving perfectly square corners on the work (see Figure 6). The second type, for the finish cut, leaves a slight bevel to the edge (see Figure 7). Depending on your supplier, the bevel will vary, but it will be close to 25°. Both cutters are guided by a small ball bearing that rolls along the edge of your work.

## THE LAMINATE TRIMMER

The laminate trimmer is a small router specially modified for working with plastic sheet. It includes an adjustment that allows for both the flush cut and the bevel cut without the need to change cutters. It also provides adjustment for the depth of the cut.

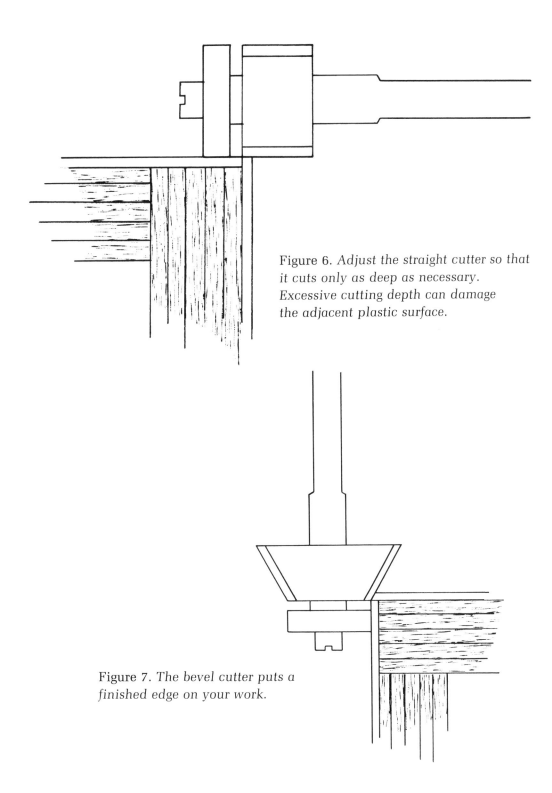

Figure 6. *Adjust the straight cutter so that it cuts only as deep as necessary. Excessive cutting depth can damage the adjacent plastic surface.*

Figure 7. *The bevel cutter puts a finished edge on your work.*

## THE NONPOWER TRIMMER

The hand trimmer, like the power trimmer, cuts the plastic accurately by guiding along an adjacent edge (see Figures 8 and 9). But instead of cutting the plastic with a rotating tool, it scores it with a carbide-tipped scribe. The cutter is run back and forth until the material is scored below the depth of the decorative or colored layer, then the plastic is broken upward toward the face. Although this may sound too easy to do a good job, the hand trimmer can produce a surprisingly good edge and is used by many

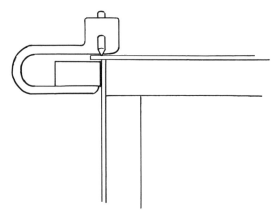

Figure 8. *The hand trimmer scores the plastic precisely. The excess material is then snapped off.*

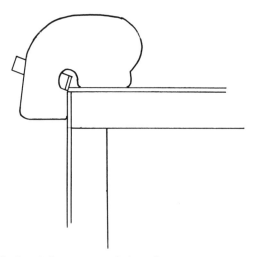

Figure 9. *The angled blade of the Mica Nife hand trimmer puts a slight finishing bevel on the edge.*

professionals in spots too cramped for the larger power tools or where power may not be available. You must be careful, though, to run the hand trimmer back and forth precisely so that the scribe stays in the one scored line. If you let it wobble and begin to produce two or more scored lines, your break will not be true.

## COMPLETING THE CUBE

Let's demonstrate all these steps now by completing the cube (see Figure 10). Begin by cutting the plastic for the two C sides. (In fact, you'll probably cut all the plastic pieces at once, and if you're producing a perfect cube, they'll all be the same size, unlike the plywood components.) Whatever your dimensions, cut the plastic about $\frac{1}{2}''$ oversize at each edge, or 1" extra over-all.

Apply the adhesive, let dry adequately, then apply the two C sides, leaving even margins all around.

If you are trimming with a router, make the first "rough" cut with the straight cutter. It will appear that the plastic is flush on all sides, but actually the placement of the cutter and the roller guide allows a lip of a few thousandths of an inch to remain.

If you are using a laminate trimmer, adjust it to make a straight cut and to leave a small lip, perhaps $\frac{1}{16}''$ or so. The hand trimmer is not adjustable but will leave the slightest lip.

Now sand these lips flush with the edges. Using a medium-grit sandpaper or belt, begin your sanding pass at one end of the work and continue across and off the other end. Next, begin at the opposite end and continue across and off. Moving the sander in such a pattern helps keep the edges true. If you just move the sander around until the lips are removed, you very likely will have sanded a "belly" into the work.

When the sanding on the C-face plastic is complete, add the plastic to the B faces. At the top and bottom of the B faces—that is, where you are still guided by wood surfaces—rough-cut and sand as you did on the C faces. But on vertical edges, plastic now meets plastic and you can't use the sander. Make first a rough cut, using the straight bit on the router or adjusting the laminate trimmer for a slight lip.

These, and all succeeding edges, can be left at 90° or can be beveled, although the bevel is better for furniture. If you used the router and straight bit, the tiny lip is not apparent to the eye, so the face can be considered finished.

To accomplish the bevel cut with a router, adjust the cutting depth so that the angled cutting edge just touches the plastic, removing insufficient material. Then, ever so slightly, increase the cutting depth and test it on the edge. Continue slight increases until the cut is correct.

If you are using a laminate trimmer, set it for the bevel edge but, again, to remove insufficient material. Adjust in tiny increments until the cut is correct.

If you have used the hand trimmer, it will also have left a slight lip. Now, using a companion tool, the Mica Nife (see Figure 9), draw the cutting edge across the plastic

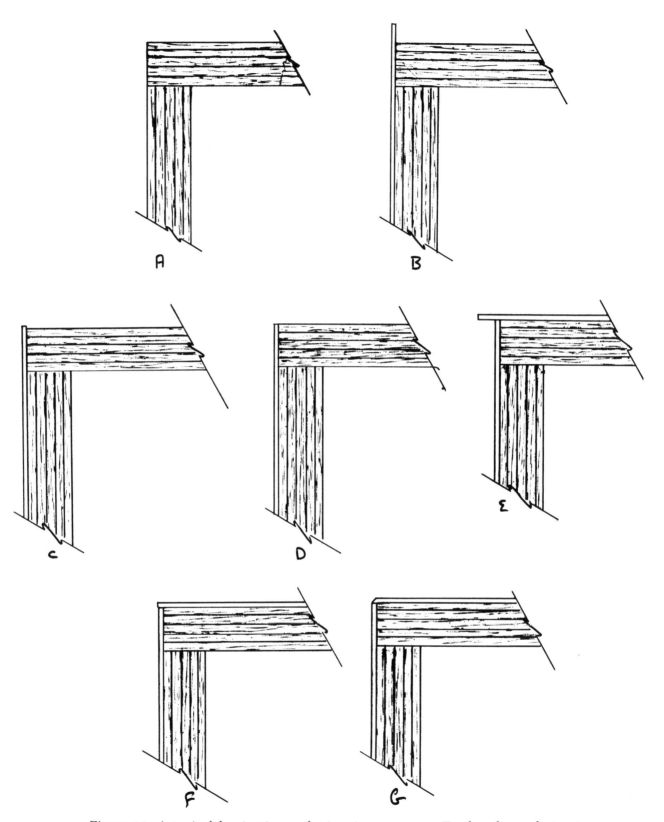

Figure 10. *A typical laminating and trimming sequence. To the plywood structure (A) is added the vertical plastic surface (B). The excess plastic is trimmed away (C), leaving only a tiny lip, which is then sanded smooth (D). The top surface is then added (E), trimmed (F), then finished with a bevel (G).*

until the edge is smooth. The tool can't be adjusted for a 90° corner but can be adjusted for varying degrees of bevel. (See Buyer's Guide.)

The last step is applying the top. It is finished with all machine cuts. Finish the four edges as you did with the preceding plastic-to-plastic edges. Check each cut before going on to the next one to see that your machine hasn't slipped out of adjustment. It can if you don't tighten your setting sufficiently, and there is nothing more frustrating than to get to the end of a lovely piece and spoil an edge.

When all trimming is complete you will want to "ease" the edges with fine sandpaper. A freshly cut plastic edge can cut you and needs to be dulled a bit. Use a sanding block for better control; you want only to touch the edge.

## THE ALUMINUM SYSTEM

The AMCO enclosure system (see Buyer's Guide) was originally developed for the construction of electronic instruments, computer components, laboratory equipment, and such. It consists of a series of aluminum castings and hollow tubing that lock together with spring fasteners.

The system is available in two sizes, $\frac{3}{4}''$ and $1\frac{1}{2}''$. The lighter scale is appropriate for smaller tables, legs for cabinets, and similar light-duty applications. The heavier system serves for seating pieces, larger tables, and other applications where the system must support greater weights or resist flexing. Use of one or the other size in the designs to follow will serve as a guide in determining which one to use in any designs of your own.

The tubing is extruded from high-strength aluminum aircraft alloy, so a given size is considerably stronger and more rigid than the same size of aluminum that you may be familiar with. The castings are precision-cast and quite uniform.

The clips that lock the castings and tubing together fit into recesses in the casting and exert pressure against the inside of the tubing. Permanent fasteners have barbs that function somewhat like those of a fishhook. And they work! Once in place, the components can't be separated without destroying them. For this reason, the "temporary" fasteners, with no barbs, are recommended for the amateur. In practice, they hold almost as securely as barbed fasteners and allow you to take the structure apart and start all over again if you make a mistake. To gain maximum strength, apply an epoxy adhesive inside the joints.

Because most structures form a "closed circle," they must be assembled in the proper sequence. To illustrate, in your mind's eye assemble from tubing and castings a simple square, piece by piece, until you have only to add the last corner casting. There's no way to get it in (see Figure 11). The proper sequence would be to assemble the tubing and castings for two opposite sides of the square, then complete the assembly by joining them to the remaining two sides.

In practice, assemble your completed structure *without fasteners* the first time.

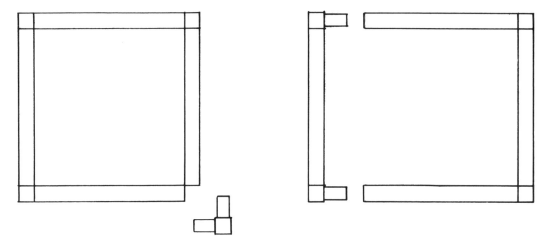

Figure 11. *The assembler of the square at the left has painted himself into a corner, leaving no way to add the last component. Plan your assembly so the components go together in patterns such as that at the right. And it's always best to rehearse your assembly pattern without the fasteners.*

Then, for final assembly with fasteners, proceed *exactly* as before. It's best to make notes.

The spring fasteners are pretty stiff and don't let the components slip together easily. You'll have to tap them together with a plastic- or leather-faced hammer, or a conventional steel hammer on a block of wood. Although this is high-strength aluminum, a direct hammer blow will mar its surface.

There are three basic finishes for the metal system. Your local electroplater (look in the Yellow Pages) can chrome the structure. It's a better-looking job if he can do the plating after assembly, but in some cases that won't be possible.

You can also polish the material to a pretty high finish with home polishing equipment, a buffer on a $\frac{1}{4}''$ drill. You can't obtain the mirror finish that chrome plate provides, but you can get something of the same effect. If you intend to polish the piece, be particularly careful to avoid scratches or other surface damage. Even minor damage makes polishing much more of a job. And be sure to polish all the tubing *before* assembly.

The most satisfactory finish for the home craftsman is brushed satin. At the beginning, the material is too tough for such things as steel wool, so you must use a rotary wire brush (a dollar or so at a hardware store) in a $\frac{1}{4}''$ drill. Here, too, you must finish the tubing before assembly.

Keep all the texture—the brush marks—in the same direction, leaving the effect of a soft miter at the corners. When your brushing is completed, you may find that the marks aren't entirely uniform. At this point, you can even it all up with steel wool.

With both polished and brushed finishes, apply a coat of paste wax *immediately* after finishing.

If you can't find the aluminum castings and tubing locally, write the manufacturer (see Buyer's Guide) for the name of a local distributor. If none exists, the manufacturer will ship your exact order, with tubing cut to the lengths you request. Ask for the complete catalog and instructional material.

The $\frac{3}{4}''$ tubing can be successfully cut with a hacksaw in a miter frame or in the special frame sold by AMCO. Don't attempt to hold it in the frame by hand; use a clamp.

Don't attempt to cut the $1\frac{1}{2}''$ tubing yourself unless you have a table or radial-arm saw. Use a *sharp*, preferably new blade. Because this is a much harder aluminum than you're probably used to, feed it into the saw much more slowly than you normally would. If you go too fast the saw simply won't take it and will come to a jarring halt!

And never go near a metal-cutting job without protective goggles!

After sawing, deburr the inside of the tubing with a file or deburring tool. Leave the deburring of the outside until after assembly to make a less visible joint.

## PLEXIGLAS

Unlike the case of plastic laminates, there is a great deal of splendid how-to-do-it material available from Plexiglas dealers or from the manufacturer at nominal cost (see previous discussion and Buyer's Guide). I will tell you here a little about what to expect in working with the material and how to go about planning your projects.

The first thing is to be sure that you are using what you think you're using. As mentioned earlier, someone not familiar with Plexiglas might well sell you something else, most likely polystyrene sheeting. There is a simple way to be sure what you are getting. Plexiglas is covered completely on both surfaces with pressure-sensitive (peelable) brown paper on which is printed the word "Plexiglas." No way to be confused.

This paper, however, serves far beyond the purpose of identification. It remains on the sheet during all operations prior to final assembly. Obviously, it protects the surface while you bang it around the shop. It also prevents the saw kerf from gumming up with softened plastic while it is being sawn. And it prevents the buffing wheel from softening sharp edges and affecting the luster close to the edges.

There are two general classes of Plexiglas, the thinner sheets, which you can easily work at home, and the heavier sheets, which you can work at home in limited ways.

As you're likely to have less to do with the heavier materials, those over $\frac{1}{4}''$ thick, we'll dispose of them first. You are most likely to use the thick materials for tabletops. Although your dealer is almost sure not to have it in stock, he can order it from his source and it will be available in a few days. You can compute the cost roughly from the stock he does have. If $\frac{1}{4}''$ goods cost $2.50 per square foot, $\frac{1}{2}''$ material will cost about twice as much, and so on.

It's not practical to cut the heavier plastic yourself unless you have expensive carbide-tipped blades, but that's academic. Order *exactly* the size you need. At those prices you can't afford to have any scrap anyway.

The material will come with a saw-cut edge. You can complete the polishing yourself.

## THE THINNER MATERIALS

You can perform all operations yourself on the thinner Plexiglas sheets, $\frac{1}{10}''$, $\frac{1}{8}''$, and $\frac{1}{4}''$. The manufacturer and many people who work in the material recommend scribing and breaking the thinner sheets. Scribing and breaking is fine for the $\frac{1}{10}''$ and $\frac{1}{8}''$ goods, but I find it less than satisfactory in most cases for $\frac{1}{4}''$ plastic. The reason: It takes only a quite shallow cut for the lightweight plastic, very much like the tiny scratch a glass cutter puts on a piece of window glass. One tap, and a clean break. But this is not quite true with the $\frac{1}{4}''$ material. By the time your scribe has plowed deep enough into the $\frac{1}{4}''$ material to insure a clean break, the cut has gotten pretty wide too. So, instead of having two perfect 90° corners at your cut, one is beveled a bit. This, of course, can be sanded smooth and square in the next operation, but it also slightly reduces the size of the piece. Sometimes this creates a problem, sometimes not. If you can, use a saw on the $\frac{1}{4}''$ material.

When you do scribe any thickness of material, try to practice a little on a piece of scrap.

If you ever built little plastic model airplanes or automobiles, you remember that the whole thing was booted if you got a little adhesive where it wasn't supposed to be. Those perfect surfaces were spoiled, with no way to repair them.

It would seem, at first glance, that the same would be true of Plexiglas. It's not. If you should get a drop of the adhesive or solvent on the plastic surface during application, you have three or four seconds to wipe it off without any serious visible damage. If you don't see it soon enough and some damage does result, it can still be buffed away. The buffed spot can be seen with perfect lighting conditions, but for practical purposes, it isn't visible.

Because of its relatively high cost—higher than plywood, that is, but not high enough to put it out of anybody's reach—you'll want to plan your purchase carefully. Clear $\frac{1}{4}''$ material, for example, is available in sheets of 18″ × 24″, 20 × 32, 24 × 48, 26 × 26, 28 × 30, 30 × 34, 30 × 36, 32 × 40, 36 × 36, and 36 × 48 and can be special-ordered in larger sizes. Careful planning both at the design stage and when you purchase the material can result in little or no scrap, minimizing your costs.

There are specialized tools available at the dealer's for working in Plexiglas. I guess you could devise other ways of doing the job, but you're better off using these tools. They're not expensive, and they make the job easier and reduce the likelihood of trouble. The drills, for example, are for plastic and help eliminate cracking in the holes that might be caused by metal-working drills.

The strip heater, which is used for bending relatively sharp corners in the material, calls for the construction of a simple holder from plywood and asbestos paper. The holder takes only a few minutes to put together. Before you start to bend a piece of plastic on the strip heater, practice with a bit of scrap. If you bend the plastic before it is hot enough, there will be stress cracking in the bend. If it gets too hot, the material will likely scorch. Let your heater get to maximum heat, then time your tests with the second hand of a watch. When everything is down pat, use exactly the same timing on the actual piece.

# Chapter Four

# SEATING

Among home furnishings, your seating pieces—the sofas, chairs, hassocks, benches, padded platforms, rockers, and such—are most readily visible and therefore best express your taste and the life-style of your family. While all the pieces here are in the contemporary vocabulary, they offer a broad spectrum of style and function. All can stand alone as a single piece of furniture. Some can be repeated indefinitely, providing a long wall of seating if your room calls for it. Some can be used in combination to form "conversation pits," recently rediscovered by interior designers, or to turn corners against your wall if need be (see Figure 12). All can be made in either sofa or chair versions.

Aside from a few basic dimensions—comfortable seat heights and depths, for instance—the size of any piece can be varied to suit your needs. If a $7'3\frac{1}{2}''$ sofa is what you need to fit a particular space, by all means build it to that size. Standard dimensions for the mattress that will serve as your "upholstery" are $5\frac{1}{2}''$ thick, 39" wide, and 75" long for a conventional twin, or 39" by 80" for an "extra long" twin. But both latex foam rubber and urethane foam are available in a variety of stock sizes or can be custom-cut to your own specifications. If you have no convenient local supplier, stock sizes are available by mail from Sears, Roebuck.

Most of the sofa designs shown here use a $33'' \times 75''$ latex foam rubber mattress.

A typical sofa or lounge chair seat is 15" or 16" off the floor and from 24" to 30" deep. The 33" mattress width is reduced to the 24" seating area by the addition of a back bolster or pillows or both. As a rule, because of its effect on your seating posture, a lower seat should also be a little deeper. Measure the seat dimensions of an existing sofa or chair and develop your ideal dimensions from that. If you are particularly tall or short and have always found that commercial sofas or chairs are designed for somebody else, now's the time for one that fits *you.*

When planning any larger piece of furniture, remember that lumberyards generally stock no longer than 10' plywood. If the seating platform on a sofa, for example, is any longer, it must be built of two pieces of plywood and you will have to provide adequate support at the joint. Too, longer pieces have a way of not going up stairs or around corners when you try to move them. (Remember the old cartoon about the man who built a boat too large to take out of his basement?)

Unless you special-ordered your plastic laminate, it will be only 8' long and 4' wide. Any greater dimensions on a single surface will call for a joint in the plastic.

When it's necessary to make a plastic joint in a highly visible spot, try to use the "machine edges," the factory-cut edges of the material, because they are generally better than any you can cut with home equipment. Be sure to check them for chips and straightness. Most brands of plastic are furnished a bit oversize in both dimensions, so you can cover a full 4′ × 8′ panel and still have a little bit to trim. But the color doesn't always come out to this edge on all sides, so check your edges carefully. When you make a joint, be sure it is symmetrical, exactly in the center or dividing the surface into thirds or quarters or whatever. Joints in white or light colors are most obvious; darker colors tend to hide them better. Joints made in the direction of the grain in wood-grain patterns are almost invisible.

The foam seats and bolsters are covered with the simplest box slipcovers, which can be zippered if you want but needn't be. Whatever corners are to be visible in the finished piece should be welted. Your fabrics can range from dollar-a-yard goods on up. This kind of furniture is also complemented by leather upholstery. And while real leather upholstery is pretty classy and expensive and might defeat your whole purpose, one of the new poromeric materials, Rucaire, has the look and feel of leather at a small fraction of the cost, and what's more, can be sewn on your home machine. (See Buyer's Guide.)

## THE SOFA

There are four basic wood-and-plastic sofa constructions. They all achieve the same thing—a structurally sound shape on which to apply the plastic—but the steps

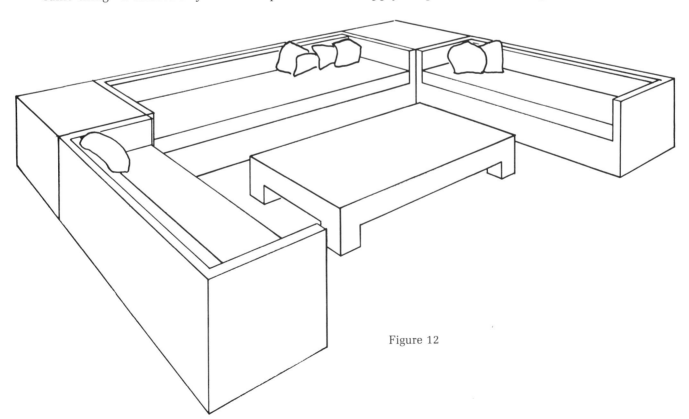

Figure 12

vary a bit from type to type. None is more or less complicated than the others. They all call for a minimum number of plywood components assembled with nails or flathead screws, nothing more. In most cases throughout this section, I will refer to "the sofa." Feel free to substitute "the chair." The steps are the same.

## THE BOX SOFA

The box sofa is essentially two U's, one inside the other and joined by spacers. The inside dimension of the inner U is equal to the length of your mattress. Don't begin construction of your sofa or any other piece that uses foam until the foam has arrived and you can measure it. Stock foam rubber mattresses vary as much as an inch in both length and width, and you'll want to build your piece to fit the mattress that you have. If the foam is being custom-cut, remember that your supplier isn't always perfect either.

The sofa shown (Figure 13) is 24″ high, 39″ deep, uses a 33″ × 75″ mattress, has 4″-thick arm and back sections, making the length 83″ over-all. If you intend to put the piece on casters—always helpful for a large piece of furniture—reduce the height to compensate for the casters so you don't increase your planned seat height. The casters will be mounted on caster platforms which are installed before the final lamination.

The shell of the sofa consists of six panels—two inner arms, two outer arms, an inner and outer back. Although most pieces in this book call for $\frac{3}{4}$″ plywood for major components, the rigidity of this box construction allows use of $\frac{1}{2}$″ plywood for these six panels. All other components must be of $\frac{3}{4}$″ material.

All component dimensions given are for the sofa described above. Add or subtract appropriately if your dimensions are to be different.

The first step is assembly of the two inner arms. The panels are 24″ high × $35\frac{1}{2}$″ deep. The horizontal spacers which form the tops of the arms are 3″ wide × $35\frac{1}{2}$″, and the two vertical spacers are 3″ × $23\frac{1}{4}$″. Assemble the two arms as shown in Figure 14.

The inner back panel is 75″ long and 24″ high. The horizontal spacer is 3″ × 82″, and the two vertical spacers are 3″ × $23\frac{1}{4}$″. Assemble as shown in Figure 14 with the horizontal spacer extending $3\frac{1}{2}$″ beyond the panel at both ends. The vertical spacers divide the area roughly into thirds.

While the cube table we built in the previous section had all its plastic edges on outside corners and easily accessible to the trimming tools, the inside surfaces of a sofa present something of a trimming problem. The simple solution is to laminate the inside surfaces of any sofa, cabinet, or whatever prior to assembly when all are accessible. When you apply the plastic to the inner arms and back, leave as small a margin as possible at the top and front edges so they can be sanded flush. Otherwise your router or trimmer will guide on the sawn edge of the panel. The rear and bottom edges are not visible in the finished piece, so they can be given a rough cut.

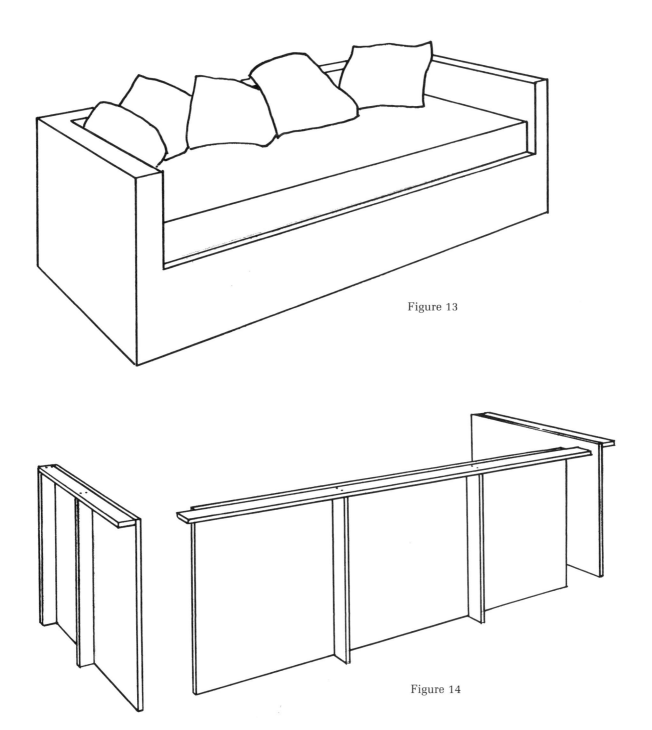

Figure 13

Figure 14

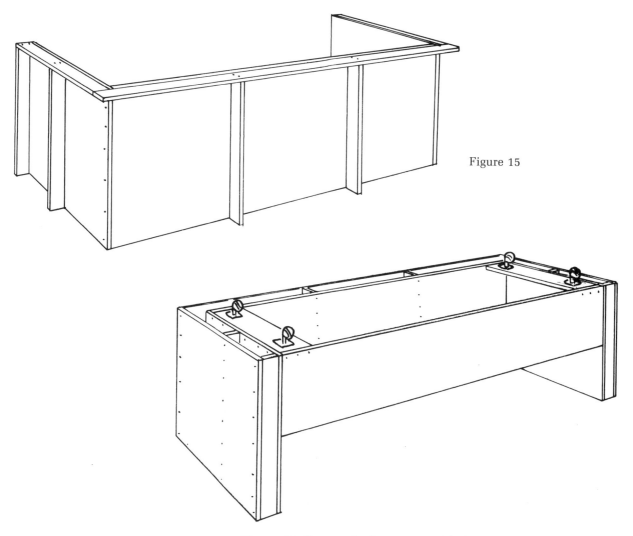

Figure 16. *Caster platforms are added before final lamination.*

When all three surfaces are laminated, assemble the components with sixpenny finishing nails as shown in Figure 15.

If the sofa is to be on casters, the platforms should be installed at this point. (see Figure 16). Cut them from $\frac{3}{4}''$ plywood, $34\frac{1}{4}''$ long and 8″ wide. Because the platforms will carry the full weight of the sofa and its occupants, they are secured to the inner arm panels and the inner back panel (and, later, the front apron) with 2″ No. 10 flathead screws. Use three screws through the back panel, six through the side panels, and, later, three through the apron.

The last step for the shell is addition of the outer panels. The back panel is 24″ high by 82″ long and is nailed to the horizontal and vertical spacers. The side panels are 24″ high and 39″ deep and are nailed to the arm spacers and edge of the back panel as shown in Figure 17. Your shell is complete.

The cleats which support the mattress platform and to which the apron is

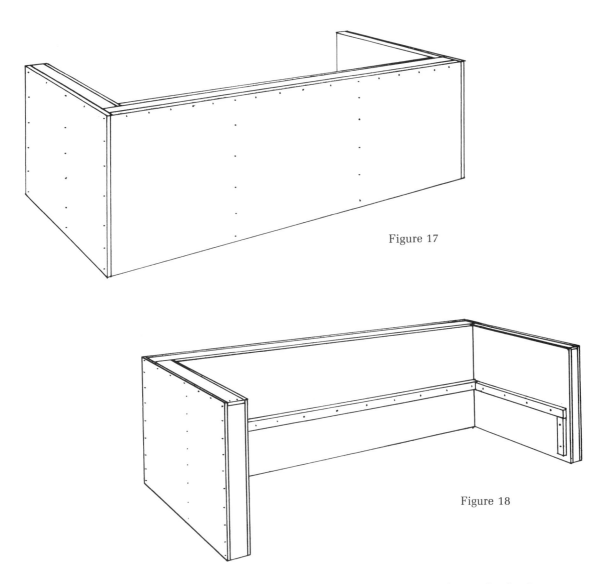

Figure 17

Figure 18

attached are now added as in Figure 18. Assuming a 16″ seat height, subtract the thickness of your mattress (in this case $5\frac{1}{2}″$) and the $\frac{3}{4}″$ thickness of the platform. The result is $9\frac{3}{4}″$, the height from the cleat tops to the floor. If you are using casters, also compensate for their height.

The vertical cleats, also shown in Figure 18, are set back $\frac{3}{4}″$ from the front to allow the apron to be mounted flush with the front of the arms. Cut the cleats approximately 2″ wide from scrap and install with $1\frac{1}{4}″$ No. 8 countersunk screws, about 8″ apart.

Secure the $\frac{3}{4}″$ plywood seat to the cleats with sixpenny finishing nails as in Figure 19. Note that it doesn't extend to the front of the arms but leaves a $\frac{3}{4}″$ clearance for the apron. Your hammerhead will be coming close to the plastic, so drive the nails with caution.

The apron is cut from $\frac{3}{4}″$ plywood, 75″ long and $11\frac{1}{4}″$ high. It is then capped with a 2″-wide strip as in Figure 20. Assemble the cap to the apron with sixpenny

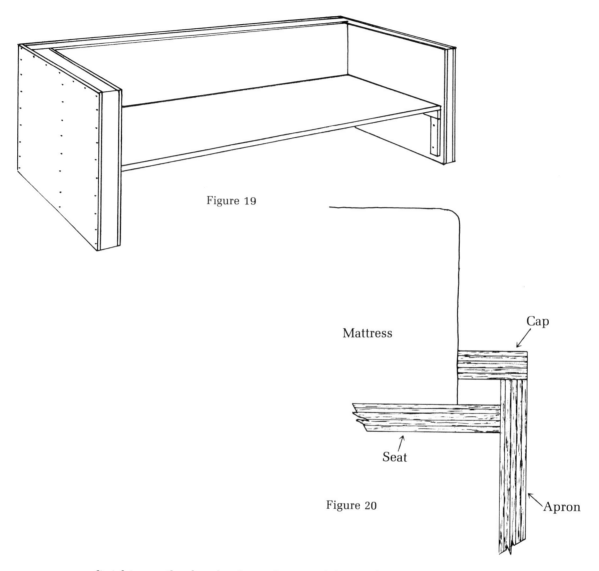

Figure 19

Mattress

Cap

Seat

Apron

Figure 20

finishing nails, then laminate the top of the cap before it and the apron are added to the sofa shell. As you did on the inner arms, leave the smallest possible margin on the front of the cap so that it can be finished by sanding. The back and the ends of the cap will be trimmed with the router or trimmer. When the plastic is being brought into contact with the cap, lay the plywood pieces on a straight table or the floor so they will be straight when they meet the plastic.

The apron is now nailed to the vertical cleats and the front edge of the seat. The seat, being for the moment unsupported in the center, may have a tendency to sag a bit. Prop it up with a scrap of wood and be sure it is straight and level before nailing the apron to it.

The shell (Figure 21) is now complete and ready for final lamination.

The front and back surfaces are laminated first, then the two ends. If you can be sure that the back of the piece will never be visible, you can save about a half-sheet of

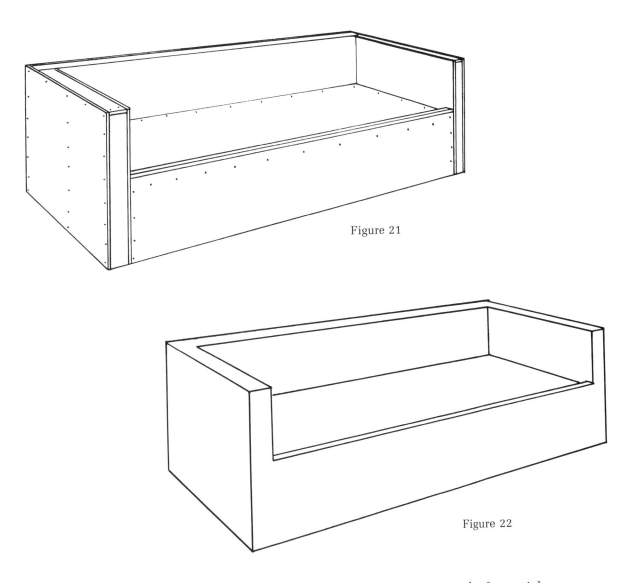

Figure 21

Figure 22

plastic by leaving it unfinished. But you are saving just a few dollars' worth of material and at some point you may regret the decision.

The top surface can be from one piece of plastic or, to conserve material further, from three strips mitered at the corners. In theory the sofa or chair is perfectly square. But it isn't, or at least not often. The saw blade wasn't adjusted to a perfect 90° angle, or one component was a bit short, pulling the piece out of square. It isn't important, your eye will never see it, but it can affect your miters.

When you cut the strips to cover the 4″ arms and back, cut them a bit wider than you normally would, perhaps 6″ wide. Lay the strip on the back and with a pencil trace the profile of the corners on the underside of the plastic. From that tracing you can lay out your 45° angles, which may in fact be 44° or 46°. Cut the miter to match this profile, and laminate the plastic to the back. Now cut true 45° miters on the strips for the arm tops and apply (see Figure 22).

## THE BUILT-UP SHELL

The built-up technique is used to achieve a thinner shell. Instead of separating the inner and outer U's with the 3″ spacers as in the box structure, the U's are separated with spacer strips of plywood in whatever combination of dimensions is needed to give you the desired shell thickness. Inner and outer U's of $\frac{1}{2}$″ plywood separated by a $\frac{1}{2}$″ spacer produce a shell thickness of $1\frac{1}{2}$″. Two $\frac{3}{4}$″ spacers provide a finished thickness of $2\frac{1}{2}$″, and so on.

Begin by laminating the plastic to the inner arm and back panels before any spacers are attached, leaving, as before, the scantest margins at the tops and fronts. Assemble the three panels into the inner U as in Figure 23, then add the spacers, back first, as in Figure 24, then ends, as in Figure 25.

If you are using only one layer of spacers, they can be attached to the inner panels before lamination as in the box method. But if you are using two or more layers of spacers, getting everything to come out even is pretty tricky, so it's easier to use the method shown in Figures 24 and 25. However, this means that you can't nail from the inside, so you'll have to be careful to use shorter nails that won't penetrate to the plastic on the inner arms. These spacers will carry no structural load, so small nails will do just fine.

After the spacers are complete, attach the outer panels — still watching the nail length — and complete like the box sofa.

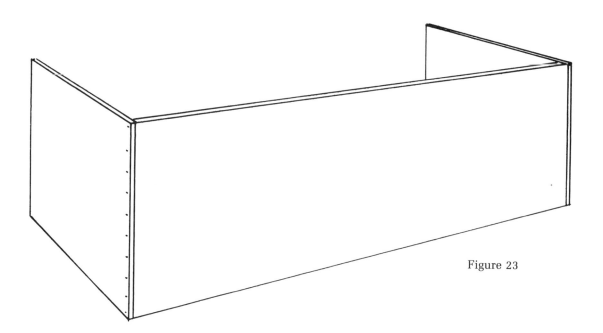

Figure 23

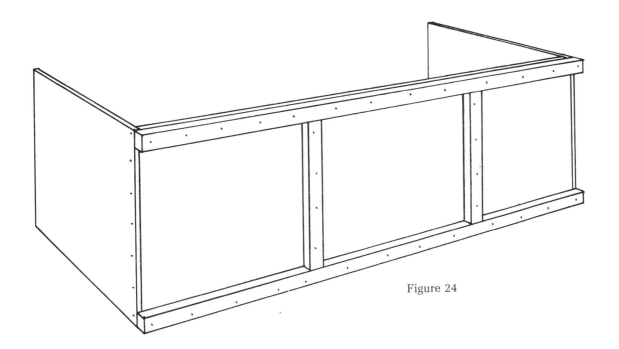

Figure 24

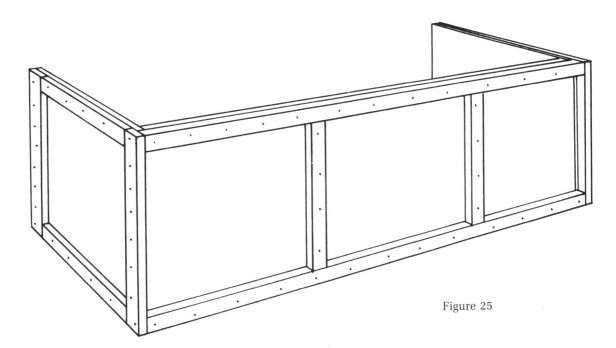

Figure 25

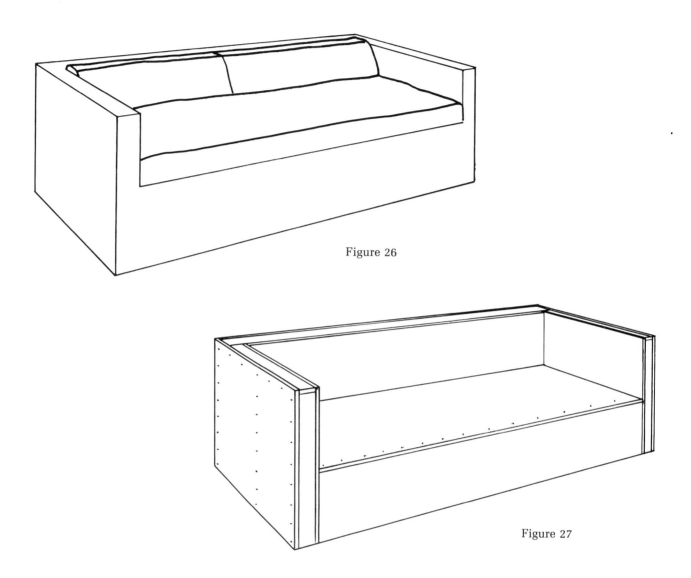

Figure 26

Figure 27

## OTHER VARIATIONS

These two basic sofa structures form the basis for a wide range of styles and "weights." Elimination of the apron lip, as in Figure 26, will bring the mattress to the front of the sofa and expose its full height. The seat is nailed directly to the apron, the apron serving as the front support of the seat, as in Figure 27. Because you eliminate the 2″ lip, remember you also reduce the over-all depth of the piece by 2 inches.

In addition to making cleaner lines for the sofa, elimination of the lip also allows you to combine two or more pieces into L- or U-shaped groups (Figure 28). Combining two or more pieces will call for the elimination of some of the arms. The only construction modification is the assembly of the armless ends, shown in Figure 29.

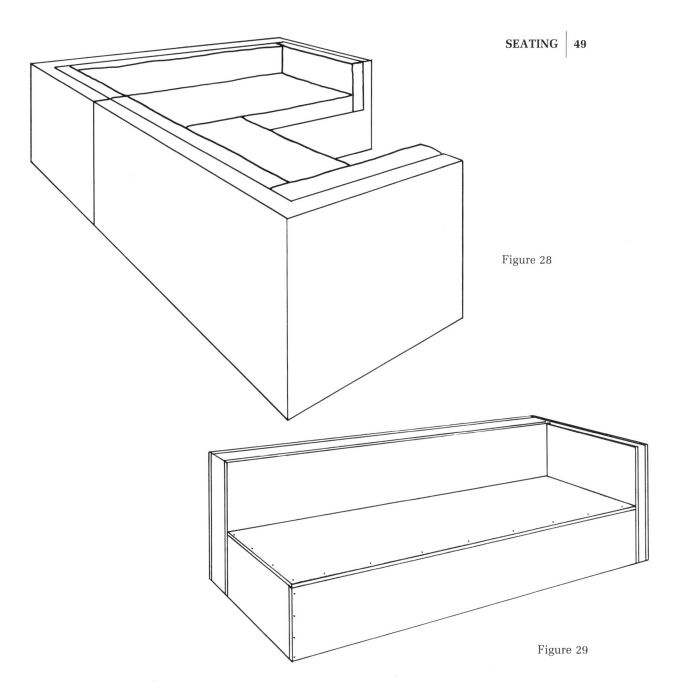

Figure 28

Figure 29

In another variation (Figure 30) of the box sofa, the apron is inset two inches, adding interest to the front lines of the piece. This, however, will call for a slightly different laminating sequence. Laminate the complete shell, arm fronts, and back first, then the sides, then the top surfaces. Attach the cleats, with the vertical cleats set $2\frac{3}{4}$ inches back from the arm fronts. Attach the apron to the seat, laminate the apron and at least the front 6 inches of the seat. The seat is nailed to the horizontal cleats as before, but the already-laminated apron is attached with 2″ angle irons at the back.

The front 6 inches of the platform are covered with plastic because, although in theory the platform is covered by the mattress, in truth it is likely to be visible here and there, particularly at the rounded ends of the mattress. There is no need, though, to put plastic on the whole surface.

Instead of resting directly on the floor or on casters, the piece can "float" on a partially or a completely hidden platform. As shown in Figure 31, the platform is quite visible and is part of the sofa's profile. A lower platform, perhaps 2″ or 3″ high depending on your taste, completely disappears under the piece. The platform may be laminated in the same color plastic as the rest of the piece, but black or a color close to the carpeting helps it disappear. The platform (Figure 32) is simply a four-sided plywood frame mounted onto members similar to the caster platforms. Mount the platform itself onto the supports before they are installed. Then, adding a third support in the center of the piece, mount in the same sequence and with the same hardware as the caster platforms in Figure 16.

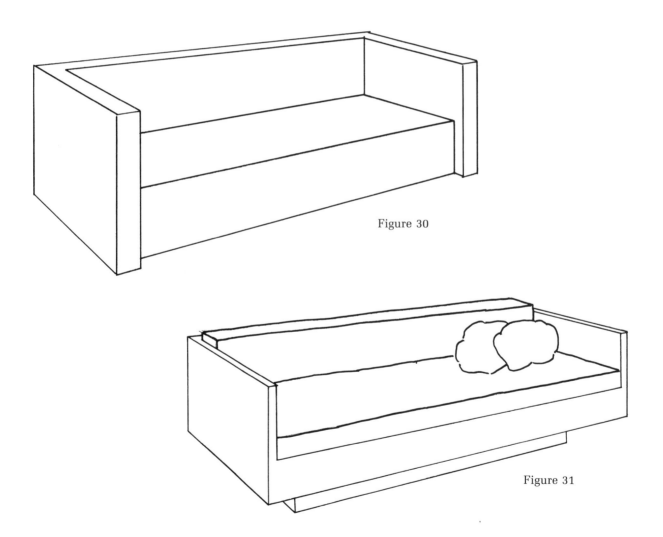

Figure 30

Figure 31

The sofa in Figure 33 is shown with a square bolster. The square bolster is most comfortable used with pillows. If you don't intend to use pillows, a wedge bolster is more satisfactory. As shown, the bolster extends 2 inches above the sofa frame, adding further profile to the piece. It may also be flush with the top. Whatever bolster/pillow arrangement is to be used, plan it in advance so that the flat seating area is 24″ deep.

Figure 33 is a built-up structure with its scale lightened considerably by elimination of the apron altogether. Begin the piece as in the basic built-up sofa by laminating the plastic to the inner panels, then assembling them into the U. The seat is mounted on a rear cleat running the full width of the piece, but because there is no apron to hide their ends, the side cleats extend only halfway from back to front. The seat is nailed to

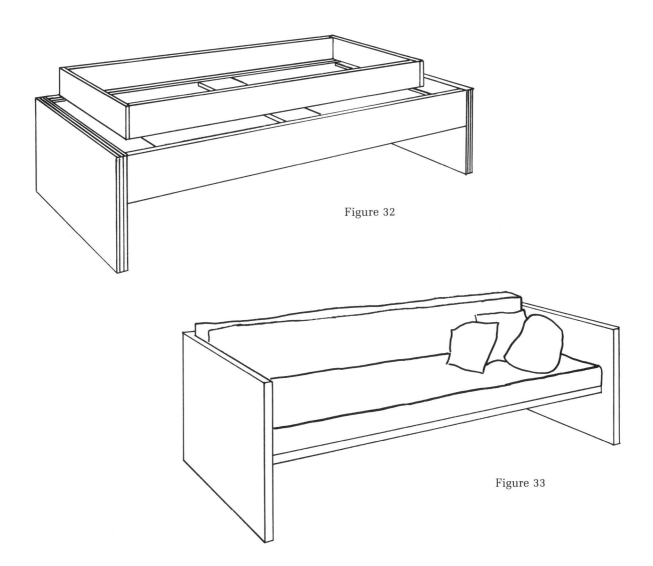

Figure 32

Figure 33

the rear cleat and half-cleats; then its front portion is secured to the side panels with $1\frac{1}{2}''$ No. 10 flathead screws three to a side (see Figure 34). To prevent any visible sag in the unsupported seat, it must be reinforced by at least two thicknesses of plywood on its underside, forming a lip. The reinforcements extend the full width of the seat and from the front of the seat back to the half-cleat. This will give an apparent seat thickness of at least $2\frac{1}{4}''$, but if your frame is thicker, the seat should be made to match. Don't try to make this style in anything less than $2\frac{1}{4}''$ thickness.

Laminate the edge and at least the front 6 inches of the seat before installation.

Because the mattress will help distribute weight—and people rarely sit in the center of a sofa—this structure should be strong enough to prevent visible sag (it's a matter of esthetics, not safety). But if the piece is subjected to excessive weights, you might want to reinforce it further with a $1\frac{1}{2}''$ angle iron tucked behind the lip and

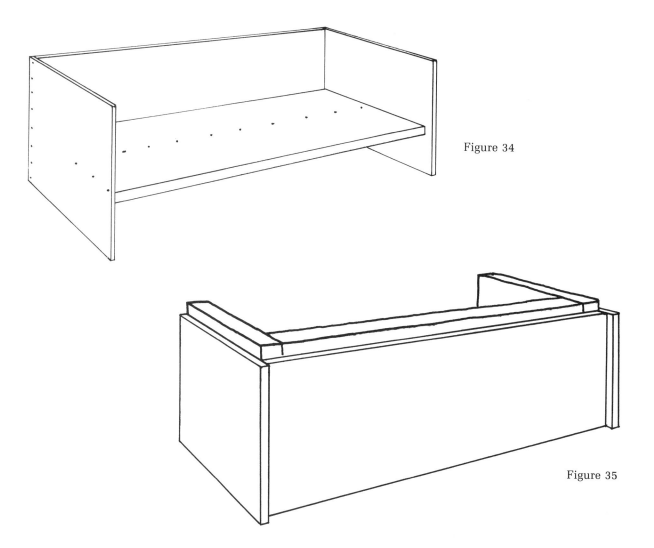

Figure 34

Figure 35

secured to the underside of the seat every 8 inches. Attach it with flathead stove bolts countersunk into the top of the seat.

After the seat is attached, continue the buildup as in Figure 24.

If the back of the piece is to be visible, there are various treatments to make it more interesting, as in Figure 35. In this case, the back buildup is completed, laminated front, back, and top, then attached to the already-laminated inner arms with No. 10 screws as in Figure 34. The arms are then completed and the sofa finished with any apron treatment desired, although a 2″ inset for the apron is most appropriate. It might also be completed without an apron as in Figure 33. Or the back can extend only below the cleats as in Figure 36. This is particularly effective in the chair version.

The sofa in Figure 37 gains dimension through use of a lip. The back and arms are a single thickness of $\frac{3}{4}″$ plywood. Laminate the inside of the three panels, then

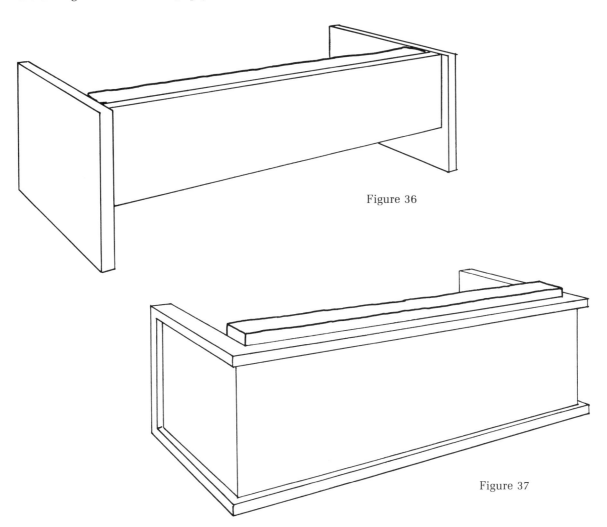

Figure 36

Figure 37

assemble into the U. Install the seat and apron, prelaminating where necessary depending on the styling. Then laminate the three outside surfaces of the arms and back.

The lip sections are then built up to the desired thickness. In this case, two $\frac{3}{4}''$ lip sections are added, yielding an over-all arm thickness of $2\frac{1}{4}''$. The first layer of lip is attached directly to the laminated outside of the shell with $1\frac{1}{4}''$ No. 8 flathead screws. Use a $1\frac{1}{4}''$ Screwmate (a combination drill and countersink from your hardware store) to prevent penetration to the plastic on the inner surfaces. When the first layer of lip is complete, attach the second layer to the first with $1\frac{1}{4}''$ screws.

The plastic goes, first, on the top of the lower lip, then, if desired, on the bottom surface of the top lip. These pieces will be mitered, and since there isn't sufficient clearance for machine-trimming, you should cut the plastic so there is just a scant margin to be made flush by sanding. Next, laminate the outer surfaces of the lip and complete the piece. With this lip construction a flush apron looks best.

Figure 38 shows a slightly different box construction. In this case, the extremely wide arms can serve as lamp or end tables. The piece has no back; the cushions rest directly against the wall.

The piece is quite simple in construction. It consists of two simple boxes forming the arms, with cleats attached to support the front and rear aprons and seat. Arrange the dimensions so the table height is about 4″ higher than the top of the mattress, in this case 14″ and 18″ respectively. Assemble the two boxes as shown in Figure 39, laminate the inside and outside of both, attach the cleats, then the aprons and seat. Remember to have at least 6″ of plastic at the front of the seat. The plastic is next applied to the front and rear of the unit, then the tabletops. Because of the width of this piece, you will almost certainly have to make a joint in the plastic on the front and rear surfaces. In this case, you might want to consider building it in wood-grain plastic. This piece can be striking with the wood grain running floor to tabletop. This will require two joints on each surface, but they will be practically invisible. If the plastic is a solid color, place the joint in the absolute center of the apron.

The piece in Figure 40 looks quite simple, and indeed it is, both in line and in construction. It consists of a seat panel of $\frac{3}{4}''$ plywood with a built-up lip giving it an apparent thickness of $2\frac{1}{4}''$. It rests on a platform secured to the seat with nails before the seat surface is laminated.

This simple piece can be built in a number of versions. The seat can be extended on one or both ends to form an end table. Or, with both ends flush with the mattress, two or more pieces can be combined to create a long wall of seating.

If the table portion is to extend no more than 24 inches it can be cantilevered out into space. End the support platform at the mattress. If the table is to be any larger it will need support, so the platform must extend under it, preferably to the halfway point of the table.

The support platform may be set 12 inches in from the front of the seat. Any further recessing might allow the sofa to tip if any great amount of weight is placed on its front edge.

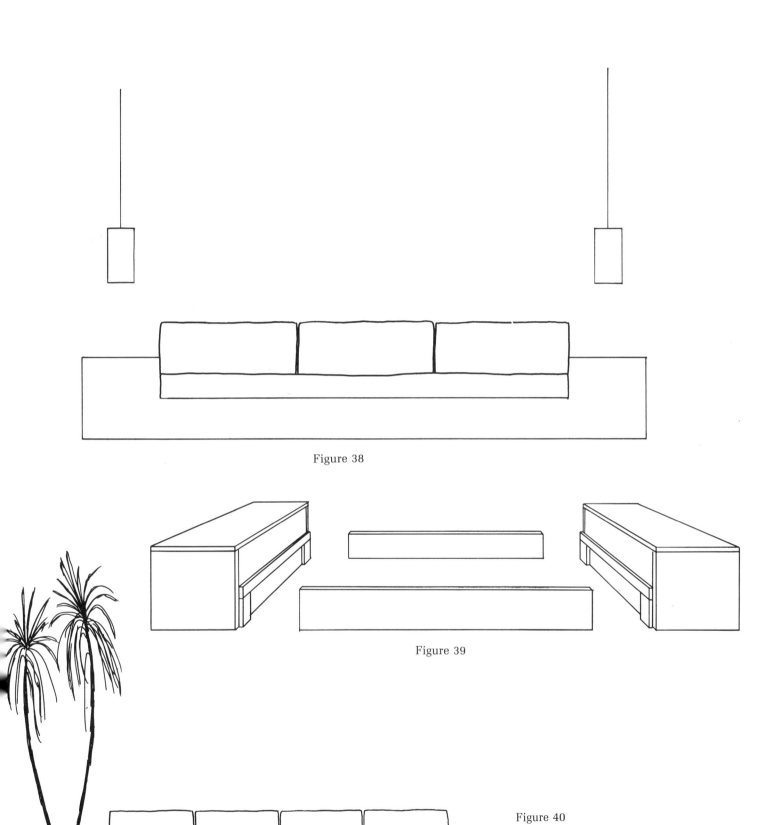

Figure 38

Figure 39

Figure 40

In the version in Figure 40 the mattress rests on the top of the seat, exposing its full $5\frac{1}{2}''$ thickness. By a build-up technique (see Figure 41), the seat can be constructed to conceal a portion of that dimension. Let the seat platform extend no more than $1\frac{1}{2}''$ to the front of the mattress or it will be tough on the backs of the knees.

If a platform sofa or chair is to be used away from a wall, a back support for the cushions must be used. Construction of the basic piece shown in Figure 42 begins with the building of the seat box, the depth of the mattress, then laminating the plastic to its top surface. Next the inner back surface is laminated and the inner back attached to the seat box with $1''$ No. 8 flathead screws. Proceed then to build up the back (see

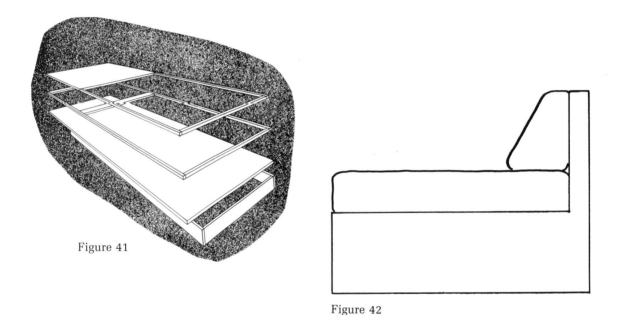

Figure 41

Figure 42

Figure 43) to its desired thickness, in this case $3''$. Laminate the front and back, then the two ends, then finally the top of the back sections.

The back support can also be added to the configuration in Figure 40. It will require however that the recessed base be flush with both ends of the seat platform, and this will become terribly complicated if you try to cantilever the tables off the ends. Your tables should be separate units as shown at the right-hand end of Figure 40.

Assemble the base and laminate its front panel. Build up your seat platform with a lip to the desired thickness, then attach to the base with nails. Laminate the inner surface of the back panel, then complete the buildup to the thickness of the seat platform. Laminate the front of the seat and the back, then both ends, finally the top of the back section.

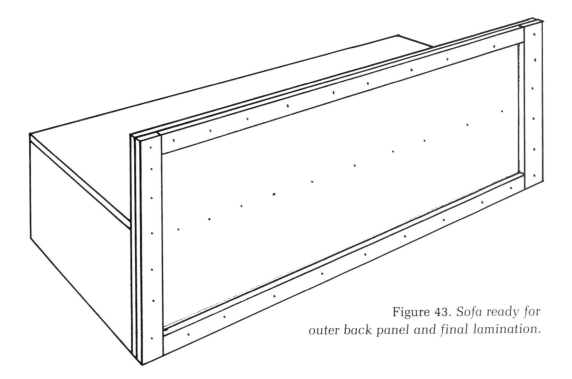

Figure 43. *Sofa ready for outer back panel and final lamination.*

## COMBINING THE ALUMINUM SYSTEM

Combining the basic plastic sofa or chair with the aluminum system can produce some striking yet still inexpensive pieces. The demands on the sturdiness of a seating piece call for the use of the $1\frac{1}{2}''$ system.

Figure 44 shows the basic sofa on the most simple metal frame. The sofa can be secured to the frame with mending plates or small angle-irons on the underside, but it needn't be. By simply attaching a block at each corner on the underside of the sofa to keep it and the frame aligned, the sofa and the frame can be kept separate, making them much easier to move or take up tight stairs or around close corners. This method has no effect on the strength of the piece.

Combining the plastic and metal calls for some attention to the proportions of the piece. Because the arm thickness and skirt height are, to the eye, the same, the height of the longer horizontal skirt should be just a little greater. In this case the arm is $4''$ thick and the apron is $4\frac{1}{2}''$ high. Because the $4''$ arm is so much thicker than the $1\frac{1}{2}''$ metal section, there need be no firm dimensional relationship.

In Figure 45, however, the sections are identical. Whereas the $1\frac{1}{2}''$ dimension and the $4''$ dimension look fine together, a $1\frac{1}{2}''$ dimension and a $1\frac{5}{8}''$ dimension would look like a mistake. So your thin sofa sections must match the metal *after* the plastic is added.

To arrive at a $1\frac{1}{2}''$ arm section, build the inner and outer arms out of $\frac{1}{2}''$ plywood and use $\frac{3}{8}''$ plywood for the build-up spacer strips. The two $\frac{1}{16}''$ plastic sheets will complete the $1\frac{1}{2}''$. The seat is $\frac{3}{4}''$ plywood with a $\frac{3}{4}''$ lip. The added $\frac{1}{16}''$ of plastic will serve to give it the same apparent thickness as the arm sections.

Construction of the sofa in Figure 46 or a similar chair calls for a slightly different structure and one procedure reversal. It begins as a built-up sofa, and its back is completed as in Figure 24. The arms, however, are a bit different. The inner arm is $\frac{3}{8}''$ plywood and is *not* laminated before assembly. Instead of using spacer strips as in Figure 25, add a second and third panel of $\frac{1}{2}''$ plywood, making the arms solid and $1\frac{3}{8}''$ thick. Because the arms carry the full weight of the sofa and its load, assemble the triple arm panels with at least twelve $1\frac{1}{4}''$ No. 8 flathead screws, equally distributed, half entering from the inside of the arm, half from the outside.

Laminate the back and the outer arms.

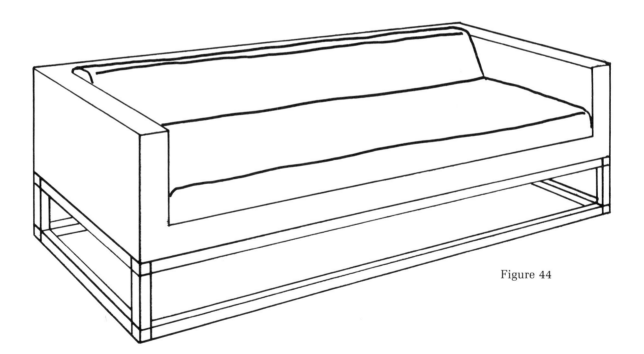

Figure 44

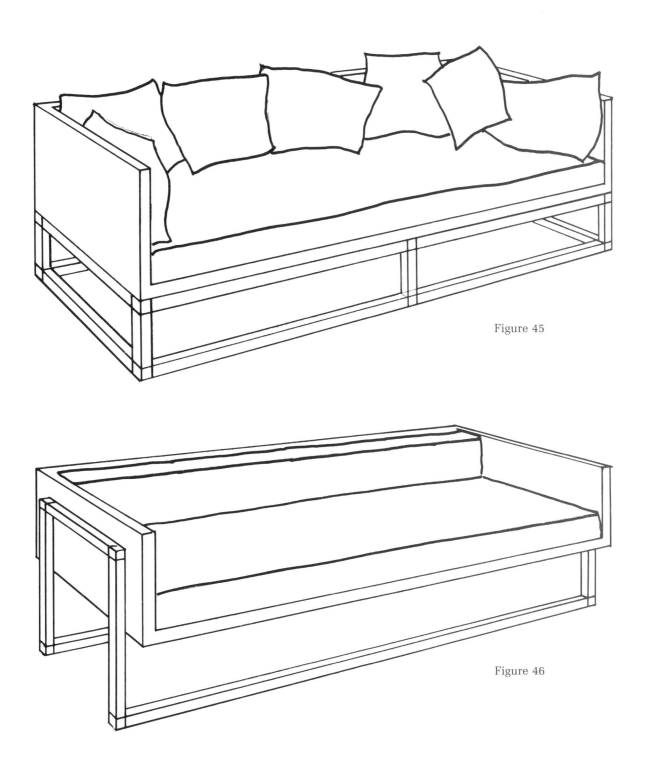

Figure 45

Figure 46

The horizontal member of the frame is mounted to the already-laminated outer arm (see Figure 47) with three $1\frac{3}{4}''$ stove bolts. Drill three holes through the arm and into one side of the aluminum tube. Be careful not to drill through the aluminum.

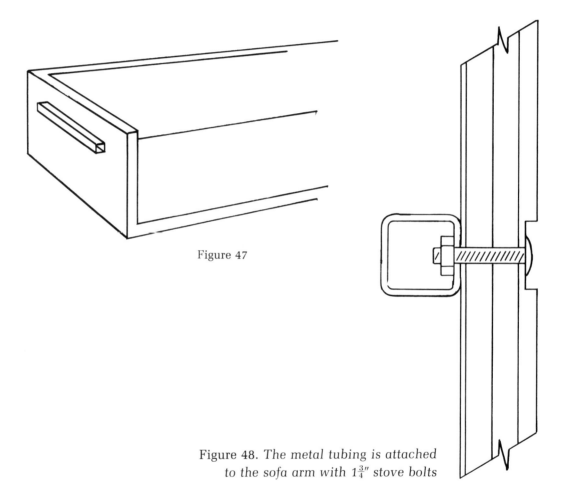

Figure 47

Figure 48. *The metal tubing is attached to the sofa arm with $1\frac{3}{4}''$ stove bolts*

The holes are located at the center and 3 inches from each end of the aluminum piece (in order to clear the casting when the vertical members are assembled to the horizontal one). On the inside of the arm, enlarge the hole just enough and deep enough to recess the bolthead (Figure 48).

Putting the nuts on the ends of the bolts inside the aluminum tube is just a bit tricky, but with a little patience and sense of humor you can accomplish it. Start by placing the center bolt through the arm and into its corresponding hole in the aluminum. Now, with a bit of double-faced tape attach the nut to the end of a long, thin stick. With a little bit of fishing around you'll be able to get the nut on the end of the bolt.

Because you can't reach in there with a wrench, jam the stick between the nut and the side of the tube so it can be tightened from the outside with a screwdriver. When tightening the center bolt, put the bolt through the hole on the far end to locate the aluminum properly. After completing the center bolt, tightening the two end bolts will come easy.

After the horizontal tube is assembled to both ends, add the four top castings, then attach the four vertical tubes that will serve as legs. Assemble the castings to the floor runners, then add to the legs. If you put the lower castings onto the vertical legs before they are assembled to the runners you won't be able to get the runners in place. As always when working with this system, assemble the piece loosely first before assembling with fasteners.

At this point, cut and fit the plastic for the inner arms. Leave very little margin at the top and front of the arms, because they will be trimmed with the sander alone. Now complete the lamination.

The little chair in Figure 49 is assembled in a similar manner except that the aluminum runs across the back of the piece. There is a single vertical support in the back (Figure 50).

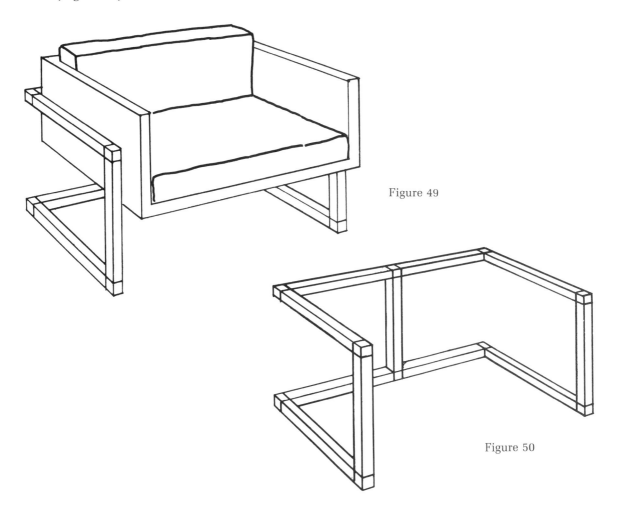

Figure 49

Figure 50

This design calls for both the inner arms and the inner back to be laminated after assembly. As with the previous sofa, first laminate the outer arms and the outer back. Attach the back aluminum tube and casting assembly with a stove bolt 3 inches from each end. Be sure the castings are properly secured before tightening the back stove bolts.

This design also calls for the outer arms and outer back to be laminated before the metal structure is attached, then the inner arms and inner back to be laminated, hiding the stove bolts. Build like the previous sofa or chair, with the seat or at least its front 6 inches laminated. Assemble the back of the metal cradle (the center casting and two sections of tube). Attach with one stove bolt in each side. Add the corner castings and the side horizontal tubes and attach with two stove bolts in each as before. Add the front castings, then assemble the three legs to their castings. Assemble the lower section of the frame, and attach the three legs to the lower section.

As before, cut and fit the inner back plastic, then the inner arm plastic, leaving only the smallest margins. Next, the arm front and the lip of the seat are laminated, then the top surfaces.

## THE ALUMINUM SYSTEM ALONE

A variety of sofa and chair designs can be built with the metal system alone. The sofa in Figure 51 and the chair in Figure 52 are built of the castings and plain tubing, except for the tubing sections that surround the seats. They are flanged tubing, the

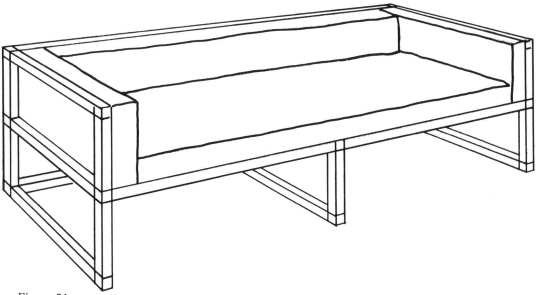

Figure 51

flanges supporting $\frac{1}{2}''$ plywood seats as bases for the mattresses. The side and back cushions simply rest against the metal frames. Because some of the softer foams aren't terribly rigid, put a piece of $\frac{1}{8}''$ hardboard inside the slipcover on the outer side of the side and back cushions. This will eliminate any tendency for the foam to "squeeze" through the openings.

Because there is no plywood sofa shell to provide additional structural rigidity, this sofa can't span the distance between ends with no center support. It will always require a center leg of some description. The top member of the back also requires center support to prevent sag (Figure 53).

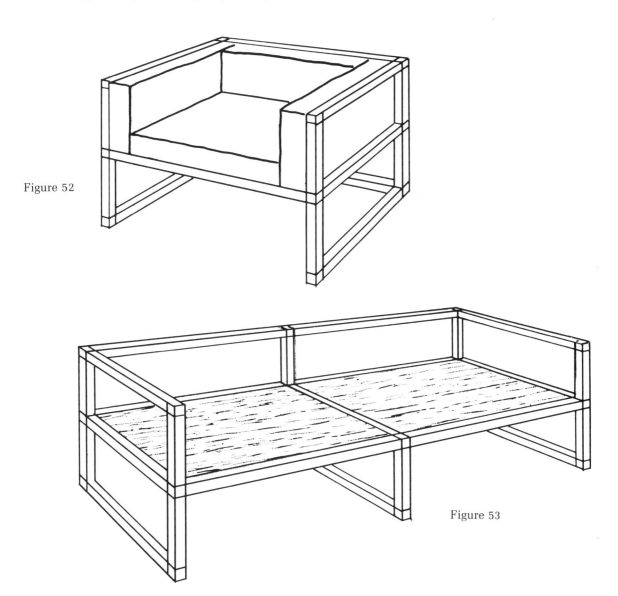

Figure 52

Figure 53

# Chapter Five

# CASE GOODS

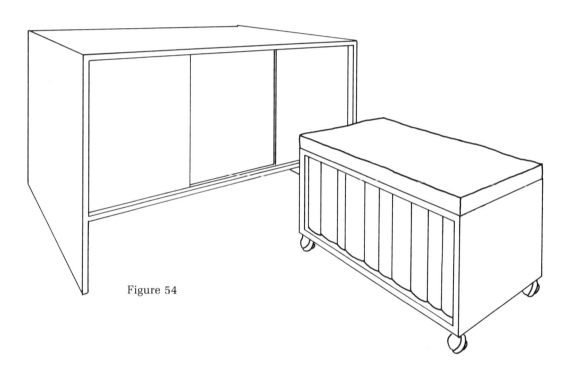

Figure 54

Cabinets and chests—in the trade they're all called "case goods"—are a necessity in virtually every room in the house and exist in a variety of forms. But all case goods here share one thing: Basically each piece is a simple box. However, by adding sliding or hinged doors, various shelf arrangements, prefabricated drawers, bins, or what have you, that box can be made to serve handsomely any storage need in your home.

All single-shell boxes are built of $\frac{3}{4}''$ plywood. Units that call for built-up sections can, like the sofas, be constructed of $\frac{1}{2}''$ material on the sides and back. All horizontal members, which might have a tendency to sag over long spans, are to be of $\frac{3}{4}''$ material.

To keep all these pieces within the capabilities of those readers with only modest —or no—experience, they have all been designed to use Rubbermaid prefabricated drawers and, in most cases, sliding doors. More-experienced builders can, of course, construct conventional drawers for any of these pieces.

## HOW NOT TO BUILD A DRAWER

It's not really difficult to build a drawer that works, but if you're not an expert it is difficult to build a group of drawers that align properly and seem right to the eye. Therefore we shall concentrate on the ways to avoid drawer building.

The simplest and most satisfactory substitute is the use of plastic prefabricated drawers by Rubbermaid. Rubbermaid drawers are available at your hardware or house-wares store. (There may be other prefabricated drawers on the market, but like the Indian rope trick, everyone seems to know about them but nobody has really seen them. In any event, they are likely to be imports that aren't distributed widely or advertised. Perhaps you will find some locally.)

The Rubbermaid drawers were originally designed to be attached to the under-side of kitchen wall cabinets and are available from any Rubbermaid dealer, although he might have to order the specific size you require. Rubbermaid Spacemaker units are $15\frac{1}{4}''$ wide and $12\frac{1}{2}''$ deep and either $4''$ or $6''$ high. They mount with screws to the underside of your chest top or shelves. Because the drawers don't pull out horizontally but drop downward a bit as they are opened, leave $2\frac{1}{4}''$ clearance beneath each drawer.

Rubbermaid also makes a series of what it calls "Slide-Out," drawers which slide out on runners very much like an office file cabinet. They are $19\frac{1}{2}''$ deep, $2\frac{3}{4}''$ high, and either $9''$, $12''$, $14''$, or $16''$ wide. There is a final version $19\frac{3}{4}''$ deep, $6\frac{1}{4}''$ high, and $9''$ wide. These pull out horizontally, so they require no significant clearance.

Another solution to the drawer problem is the use of clear plastic sweater boxes in metal frames. These are often used in retail stores for display and storage of soft goods. There are various manufacturers, and the boxes and frames will be available locally. Look in the Yellow Pages under "Store Fixtures."

Or you can simply use sweater boxes resting on shelves.

A not so highly recommended way around the drawer problem is to use the drawers and drawer frame from an old chest. Very often the frame and runners can be removed intact and you can build a new shell around them. However, this requires that the old drawer fronts can be removed and replaced with new flush drawer fronts. It's difficult to provide any specific instructions, because each case is bound to be different.

## THE SIMPLE BOX

By far the majority of your storage needs throughout the house can be met with cabinetry based on the simple box (see Figure 55). Its top, bottom, and two sides are $\frac{3}{4}''$ plywood. The back can be as light as $\frac{1}{4}''$ plywood or hardboard.

Laminate the inner surfaces of the bottom, sides, and back before assembly. To conserve material, you can eliminate the inner plastic if the piece is to have doors,

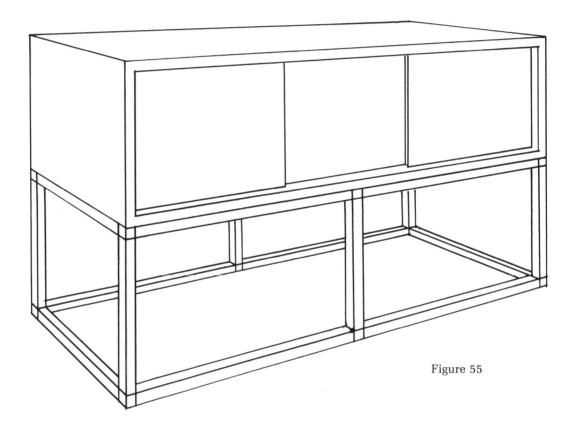

Figure 55

particularly if it is filled with a lot of drawers. Paint the inner surfaces with a hard enamel.

Fixed shelves of $\frac{3}{4}''$ plywood are laminated (first the edge, then the top surface) before mounting into the box. Install with $1\frac{1}{2}''$ No. 8 flathead screws through the sides and back.

The lamination sequence here is a bit different from that with the cube, which we did for illustration. In this case, laminate the two sides first, then the top, which is the A surface, then the front (and back, if it is to be exposed).

The front edges can be covered with a single piece of plastic, or the plastic can be mitered. If it is to be a single piece of material, saw a pretty-good-sized hole in the middle of the sheet before it is joined to the piece. This hole will make your final trimming job simpler.

You saw the rough hole by making what is called a "plunge cut." Rest the front of the sole plate of the saber saw against the plastic with the saw blade extending out horizontally (see Figure 56). Start the saw and slowly lower it until the blade comes into contact with the plastic. It will chisel out a slot. At this point you can put the blade through the sheet and saw normally. Be sure to start the cut into the underside of the sheet.

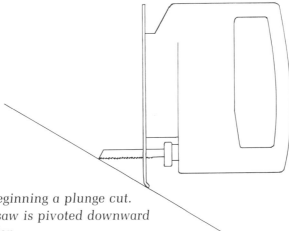

Figure 56. *The saw position when beginning a plunge cut. When the plastic is penetrated, the saw is pivoted downward until the blade is in a vertical position.*

To make a mitered front, be sure to cut your strips much wider than you need to assure yourself plenty of leeway for imperfect measuring. (See the Box Sofa, page 45.) To cover a $\frac{3}{4}''$ edge, the strips should be at least $1\frac{1}{2}''$ wide.

If the 45° miters at each corner don't seem to go together properly, your "square" box has probably warped a bit out of square. If you cut the two sides to identical heights, the top and bottom to identical lengths, you can push and shove a little and put the box back into square, making the miters fit properly. An out-of-square box generally results when the original component-cutting has not been a perfect 90°. Keep checking saw adjustments throughout any project.

The chest is now ready for doors. It's shown in Figure 55 with three approximately equal sliding doors, but your door configuration will depend on what you've done inside the chest.

With only shelves to contend with, plan to have the visible portions of the doors equal. In fact, however, the center door, which runs in the rear track, should overlap each of the side doors at least an inch on each side, making it 2″ wider. If you are using only two doors, make the one that runs in the rear track 1″ wider than the front one, to provide this overlap.

If, however, you install three stacks of drawers in the chest in Figure 55, this arrangement with a wider center door won't work. Slid all the way to either side, the center door will not completely clear the center stack of drawers, something of an embarrassment after you've completed the cabinet.

The solution is to leave a little more space between the stacks than you might normally, and reduce the overlap a little if necessary. Work it out on paper beforehand so that everything is accessible. If it is necessary to make the two outside doors a little wider than the center one, no great visual harm is done.

The doors slide in either extruded-aluminum or vinyl channels, mounted at the top and bottom of the opening. The aluminum channels can be painted to match the case, left shiny, or covered with a strip of plastic applied with adhesive to the front surface of the channels. Or they can be recessed into the structure.

Mount the channels (a hardware-store item) before you cut the doors. The cutting height for your doors, then, is equivalent to the measurement from the top inside of the upper channel to the top of the lip of the lower channel (see Figure 57). The doors are installed by fitting them into the upper channel, then swinging them into place past the lip of the lower channel, then dropping them to rest. Don't try to fit full-height doors into the channel installation, then put the whole thing into place. You may want to remove them from time to time, and they'd likely stick anyway.

If you have the equipment — a radial-arm or table saw — you can recess the channels into the top and bottom of the chest. Use a dado cutter, adjusted to the proper width, or you can make several successive passes with a conventional blade. The cuts are made after the laminate is applied.

You can also cut the recesses with your router. But don't try this unless you're experienced in using a router in wood. Trimming the plastic laminate, guided nicely along an edge by the ball-bearing roller, the router is a joy to use, and the beginner can be successful the first time. But a router bit taking a full bite into a piece of wood is something else indeed. Its feel and behavior are quite different. Although it is guided along a straightedge clamped to the work — the proper method — the machine will want to go places other than in the nice straight line you had planned. It's not really as difficult as this may sound, but practice a good deal on something else before you attempt your newly laminated component.

## THE SLIDING DOORS

Sliding-door tracks are available for both $\frac{1}{4}''$ and $\frac{1}{2}''$ doors. Plexiglas doors, either clear or opaque, are ideal. Polish the visible edges, and the doors are ready to install.

Although it's a little outside the character of this book, textured hardboards for doors can often add an interesting touch. They are available in simulated basket weave and wicker, a texture that looks very much like monk's cloth, and many other textures. The disadvantage, of course, is that the doors will need painting, something we're trying to avoid here.

Using laminated doors in the $\frac{1}{4}''$ track requires a little bit more doing, but you may want to go to the trouble for the thin silhouette. It requires use of $\frac{3}{16}''$ plywood, not commonly available. What you do is buy a sheet of very low-cost prefinished paneling, which, in most cases, is $\frac{3}{16}''$ goods. A panel $4' \times 8'$ or $4' \times 7'$ will probably cost \$3 or so at one of the lumberyards that specialize in "bargains." It's not much of a bargain for paneling, but it's just fine for your doors. Ask the dealer if he has any damaged pieces for even less money.

Apply the laminate to the visible edges first—never mind the top and bottom

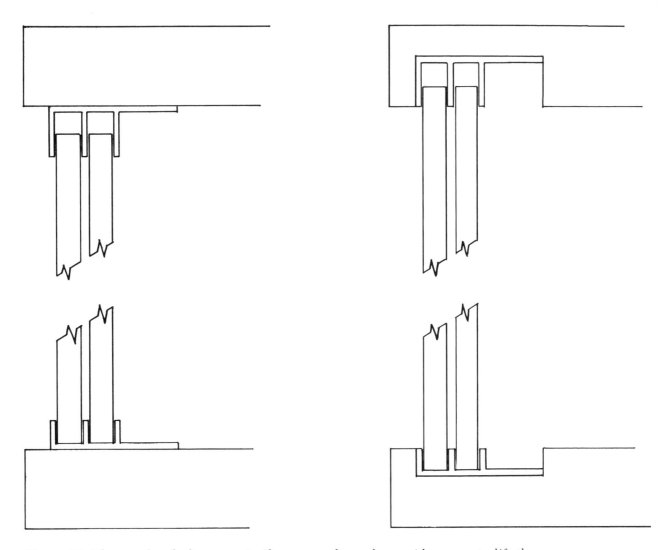

Figure 57. *The overhead clearance in the upper channels provides room to lift the doors clear of the lower channels. The channels can be surface-mounted or recessed into the plywood.*

edge. If your equipment will allow you to cut the edge strips to just over $\frac{3}{16}''$, do so. Apply to the edges and finish with the sander. Be sure the work is flat when the edges are applied.

In most cases, though, you will have to cut much wider strips, apply, rough-cut with the router or trimmer, than sand-finish. When trimming with the router or trimmer, the door should be horizontal, secured to a work surface with clamps or nails. Work carefully, because there isn't a lot of surface for your router sole plate to guide on.

The next step is lamination of the front surface of the door.

You must then apply a sheet of plastic to the back surface of the door. Although it isn't visible, it is necessary to "balance" the piece, that is, provide equal forces against warpage. Any plywood panel that is not built into a supporting structure—doors, free-floating desktops, movable shelves—must be balanced or it likely will soon be badly warped. Since your door is already $\frac{1}{4}''$ thick, the back piece covers only the part of the door that is not actually in the tracks. Leave a little extra clearance at the top for the door to slip all the way into the top track for mounting.

By far the easier method is to use $\frac{1}{2}''$ tracks. The $\frac{1}{2}''$ door consists of $\frac{3}{8}''$ plywood with plastic fully covering the front and back.

As shown in Figure 55 the chest is mounted on a $\frac{3}{4}''$ aluminum frame. It could as well be mounted directly onto the wall with lag screws. Locate the studs in your wall —they will occur every 16 inches—and attach with a $2\frac{1}{2}''$ lag screw in each stud.

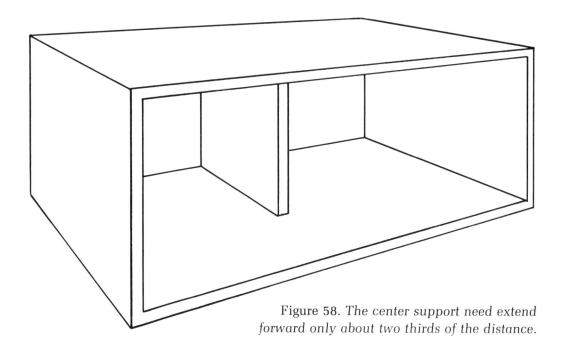

Figure 58. *The center support need extend forward only about two thirds of the distance.*

If you live in an apartment building with other than studded walls, ask your building super about mounting methods and hardware. He will very likely have definite ideas about how heavy items should be mounted.

If your chest is to be more than 5′ long, it should have a center support, separating the interior into two halves. The support should extend from the rear of the chest forward to the front edge of the shelves. If the piece will contain no shelves, the support need only extend about $\frac{2}{3}$ to the front and will thus be less readily visible. The support, of course, is to prevent sag over the long span.

As described here, the chest has a single fixed shelf, installed before the final lamination. The fixed shelf is most appropriate when it is used to support drawer units. If it is to be used simply as a shelf, mount it on shelf standards and adjustable clips—standard hardware-store items. There are two or three different styles, but you'll be happiest with the standards with the slimmest silhouette.

This case can be built with integral legs, simply extensions of the sides and back, if desired. Adding the legs calls for no change in procedure.

An alternative metal support (Figure 59) for the box is mounted like the sofa supports in Figures 46, 47, and 48 (pages 59 and 60). This is appropriate for both the large and the small aluminum system. Be sure, however, that the small system is used only with small, lightweight cabinets, perhaps for bedside use, because of the loads involved. The light system is mounted to the cabinet as it is to the table in Figure 118 (page 114).

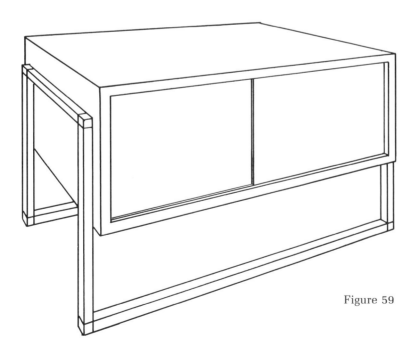

Figure 59

### VARIATIONS

There are two ways to produce chests with apparently thicker walls than the $\frac{3}{4}''$. One is the construction of a built-up shell similar to the shell sofa in Figures 23, 24, and 25 (page 46). The other method is construction of a false shell, simply adding lips at appropriate places to produce an apparent thickness. Neither is really preferable to or easier than the other. The false shell makes some compromises in appearance, visible only if the doors are open. Its advantage is that it's a little lighter than the built-up shell.

The false shell begins like the chest in the previous example with one exception. The sides and back extend below the bottom panel, creating a skirt (Figure 60). The

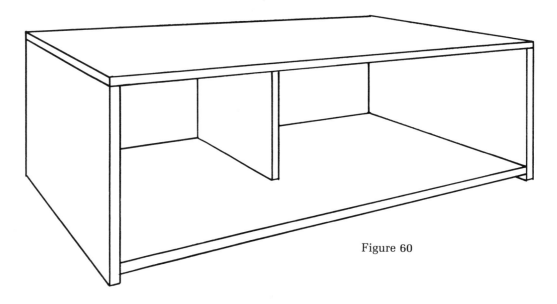

Figure 60

skirt is completed by attaching spacers under the bottom panel across the front. Spacers are then added under the top panel at the front and inside the side panels, in whatever combinations are required to create the desired thickness. (See Figures 61 and 62.)

If you are building this with integral legs, you will have to build a proper shell for the legs below the bottom panel.

Construction of the built-up chest shell begins, like the sofa shell, with a simple box. If this were to be closed with sliding doors, the fixed shelf would extend to the front of the box. This piece, however, will have apron doors, so the shelf is recessed 2 inches (see Figure 66). It is invisible when the doors are closed, so it need not be built up.

The piece shown (Figure 63) is 36″ high, 60″ wide, and 18″ deep, but the size will of course vary with your own needs. If your chest will be using prefabricated drawers, its width will depend to a great extent on the drawer arrangement.

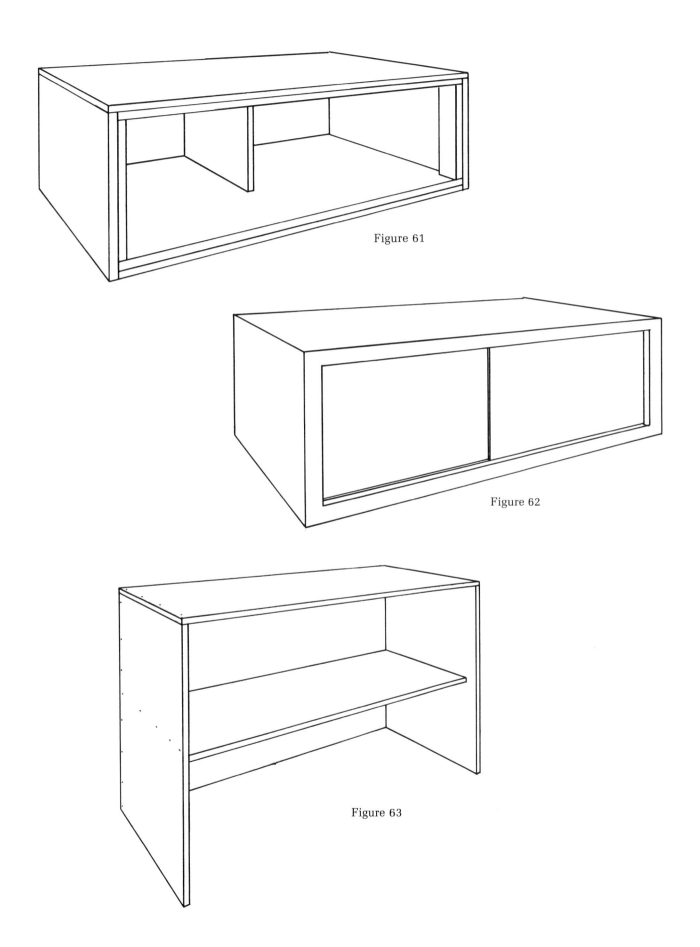

Figure 61

Figure 62

Figure 63

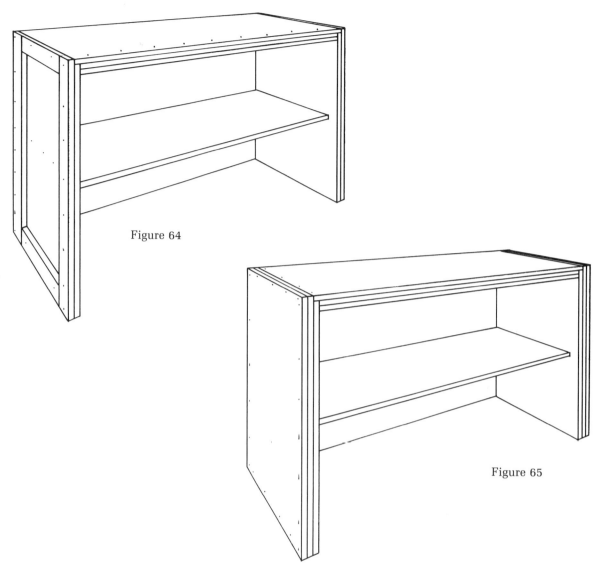

Figure 64

Figure 65

The sides are cut a full 18″ deep but only 35¼″ high. As shown (Figure 64), the built-up section consists of three thicknesses of ¾″ material, yielding a dimension of 2¼″. You may prefer to use ½″ plywood and other combinations of buildup to yield other thicknesses. If your back is to continue to the floor as shown here, it is cut to a 35¼″ height. The back can also be designed to extend just below the fixed shelf, leaving the ends to serve as independent legs. In either case, to yield an over-all dimension of 60″, the back is cut 55½″ wide.

The fixed shelf is 55½″ wide and 15¼″ deep. The top, 18″ × 57″.

Laminate the inner surfaces of the back and sides and the upper surface and front edge of the fixed shelf before assembly. The main components are assembled with six-penny finishing nails or 1½″ No. 8 flathead screws.

Add the first course of spacers to the sides and under the front of the top, forming a lip as in the false shell. Assemble the complete lip, laminate its lower surface, then attach to the structure by nailing through the top. The shell is completed by the addition of the outer ends.

Laminate first the ends, then the top, the front, and if it is to be visible, the back. The front can be either a single piece of plastic or mitered to save material.

The doors are piano-hinged directly to the inner sides and extend below the edge

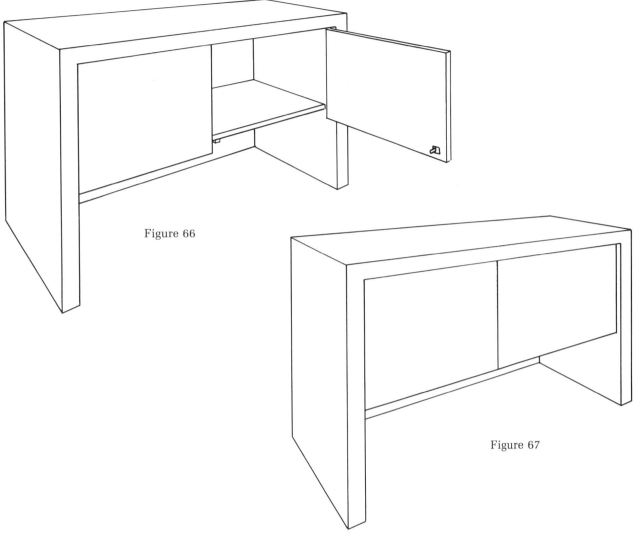

Figure 66

Figure 67

of the fixed shelf like a curtain (see Figure 66). The doors are, at first glance, the same width as the opening, but in fact, there is a lot besides the plywood to go into the space, so measure the doors carefully.

In theory the opening is $55\frac{1}{2}''$ wide. Now that it is all assembled, measure it again. Original dimensions have a mysterious way of changing as a piece of furniture progresses. Assuming that the original $55\frac{1}{2}''$ dimension held up, here's what must be subtracted to arrive at the door cutting size: $\frac{1}{16}''$ of plastic on the right and left edge of both doors, or a total of $\frac{1}{4}''$ of plastic; at least $\frac{1}{8}''$ clearance between the two doors; the thickness of your two piano hinges, probably a bit less than $\frac{1}{4}''$ each; and a $\frac{1}{16}''$ shim between each hinge and the shell. Total: $1''$. So, each door will be half of the remaining $54\frac{1}{2}''$, or $27\frac{1}{4}''$. But don't cut until you have measured the thickness of your *closed* piano hinges. They will vary a good bit from brand to brand. The skirt formed by the doors can be as long as you wish; as shown (Figure 66) it extends $2''$ below the lower surface of the fixed shelf.

Cut the doors, then laminate all four edges of both. Cut the plastic with just the smallest margins so they can be trimmed with a sander. Now laminate the front *and* back of the doors.

Attach the piano hinges first to the doors, then mount onto the shell. The shell should be shimmed away from the hinge by one thickness of plastic. The shim holds the hinge away from the shell $\frac{1}{16}$ inch and prevents its moving part from rubbing against the plastic.

Complete the chest by installation of the touch latches on the underside of the fixed shelf.

A further variation in storage pieces is the simple box on casters, providing roll-around seating as well as storage. It can be finished as a front-opening case with sliding doors, simply fitted with adjustable shelves for book storage, or built with a top-opening lid for toy storage. Top each piece off with a 2″ pad.

If these pieces are to be used with a bed, design them so that the pad thickness is equal to the amount of mattress exposed. (See Figure 68)

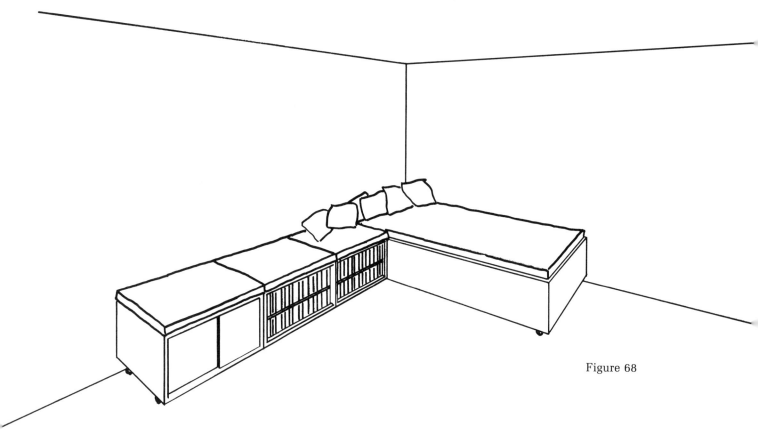

Figure 68

## A WORD ABOUT KITCHENS

While laminates have indeed gotten out of the kitchen, their value in a kitchen has surely not decreased. They resist most stains, most heat — don't, however, set a hot pan directly on a laminate — and look good for years.

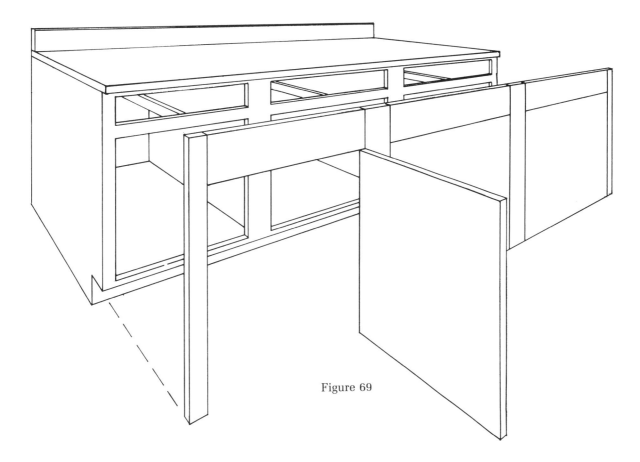

Figure 69

After the relatively complicated pieces you've seen, a kitchen counter is a cinch, and it costs a lot less when you do it than when you call in a kitchen shop. The top should be of $\frac{3}{4}''$ plywood—don't use particle board for countertops—and have a $\frac{3}{4}''$ lip, providing an apparent thickness of $1\frac{1}{2}''$. If the lip interferes with the drawers the whole top should be shimmed up until it clears.

You can laminate over an existing laminated countertop if it is sound. If it is self-edged—that is, edged with laminate—just add the new plastic and hook up the sink. If it has a metal edge as so many older counters do, remove the metal, build up the lip, then proceed.

And why stop at a new countertop? In most cases you can put new faces on all your kitchen cabinets. The technique shown (Figure 69) calls for removal of old cabinet doors and drawer fronts, then adding a new structure to the bare front of the old cabinets. Because all cabinets are a little different, you will have to solve some problems on your own, but this is in essence what you will have.

The new fronts will consist of vertical hinge boards to which you piano-hinge the doors, the doors themselves, and the new drawer fronts. Design your new drawer

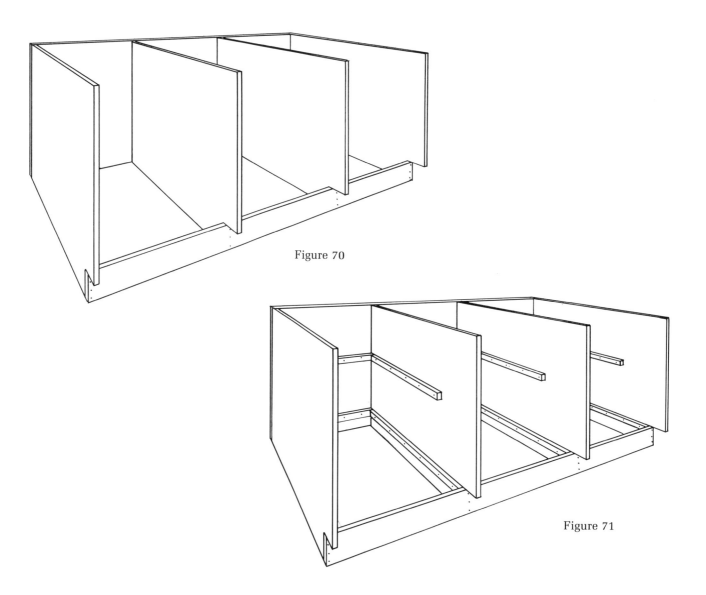

Figure 70

Figure 71

fronts so that they cover the piece of wood that separates the drawer opening and cabinet opening on your old cabinets.

All these components must be laminated on all four edges and on the front and back. They are fastened to the old cabinets by flathead screws through the old cabinet fronts.

When you're planning the new fronts, don't just assume that your old cabinets are straight and true just because they seem that way. They may have warped or the floor may have sagged a bit. Shim the old cabinets so that they will match the new faces perfectly.

Or build your own cabinets. Again, if you're an experienced builder, construct conventional drawers, but you can build as much utility into the cabinets by ignoring the drawers and using the wide variety of Rubbermaid drawers and organizers.

Begin by cutting the end and separator panels, typically $23\frac{1}{4}''$ deep and 32''

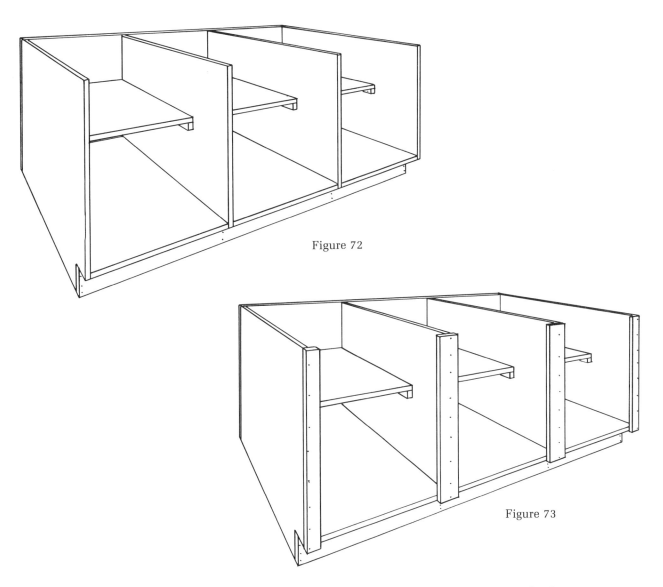

Figure 72

Figure 73

high. Cut in a toe space, 4″ high and 4¾″ deep. Assemble the panels to a common back and kickplate. Laminate all inside surfaces before assembly. (See Figure 70.)

Add cleats to support the cabinet floor and shelf (Figure 71). A single shelf, set back 8 or 10 inches, is most common, but you might well want to put in adjustable shelf hardware for more flexibility. In any case, the floor is fixed and permanent. The cleats for the floor are at the level of the kickplate, their tops 4 inches from the floor.

Next, add the shelves (Figure 72). If they are to be painted, they are nailed to the cleats. If they are laminated, they are fixed to the cleats with panel adhesive. Don't use white glue or similar water-soluble adhesives, because there is too much moisture in a kitchen for them to hold up. And all kitchen cabinets should be built of exterior-grade plywood, not particle board.

The doors are to be mounted on vertical hinge boards. The end boards are 2″ wide, the others 3¼″ wide and centered on the separator panels (Figure 73). Laminate

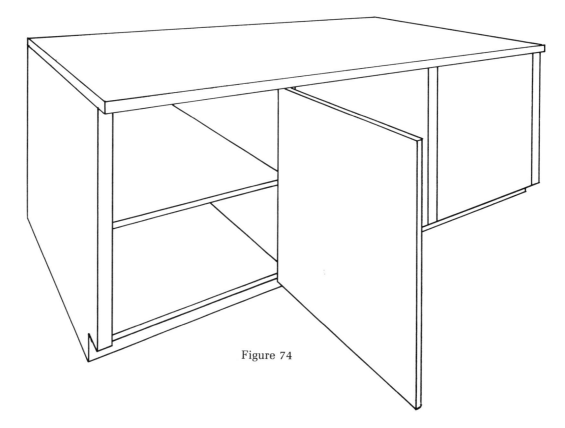

Figure 74

the backs and edges of the hinge boards and mount with sixpenny finishing nails. One exception: don't laminate the *outside* edge of the end boards. That surface will be laminated when the cabinet end is finished.

When the boards are nailed into place, laminate their fronts and the cabinet ends.

Cut the doors, laminate all four edges, front, and back, add touch latches, then attach doors with piano hinges. (See Figure 74.)

You can create a quite different kitchen look by using wall-mounted "buffet" cabinets. Those shown are simply false shells, fitted with sliding doors of smoky Plexiglas. The floor-mounted peninsula in the foreground (Figure 75) houses the sink and dishwasher.

When turning corners with laminated countertops, resist the temptation of mitering the corner unless you can saw an almost perfect line in the material. The saw cut on a mitered cabinet front is only an inch or so long, so irregularities won't be apparent. But a mitered countertop calls for a cut of three feet or so and must be well-nigh perfect to please you.

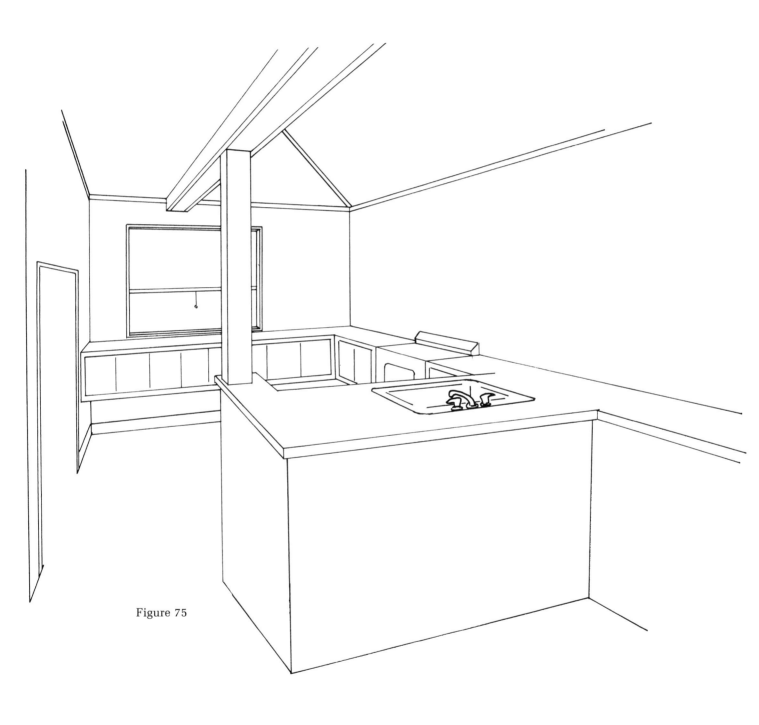

Figure 75

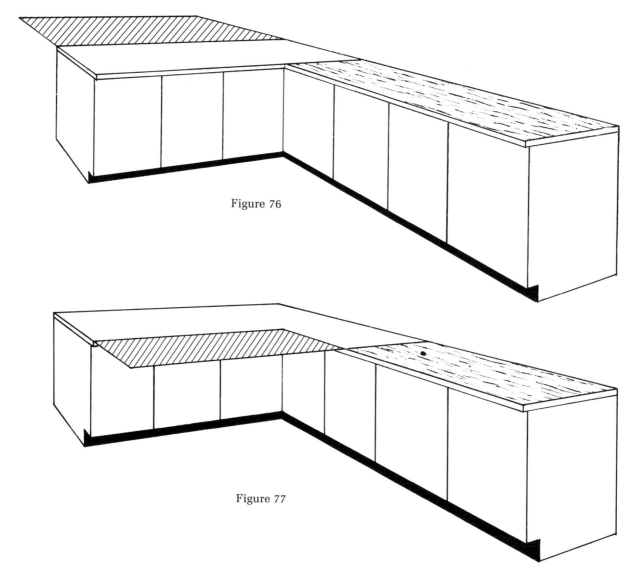

Figure 76

Figure 77

There are two alternatives, both using the machine edge of the material. One method is to use this edge as the edge of the first countertop, laying it down precisely so that it requires no trimming except the bevel cut. This machine edge continues to the adjoining wall. The short machine edge of the next sheet is butted against it as you turn the corner onto the second surface. (See Figure 76.)

Another method is to locate the machine edge of the plastic at the *back* of the first counter, letting the opposite machine edge fall 2 feet or so along the length of the second counter surface. (See Figure 77.)

Either method avoids the butting of less-than-perfect cuts.

## WALL-HUNG PIECES

Wall-mounted cabinetry offers the advantage of saving floor space while making use of space otherwise unused. Combining laminated cases and shelves with commercial shelf brackets—sometimes called "knife" brackets—and support strips, you can create an infinite variety of wall systems.

Or cabinets can be mounted directly onto the wall. Those shown offer the added

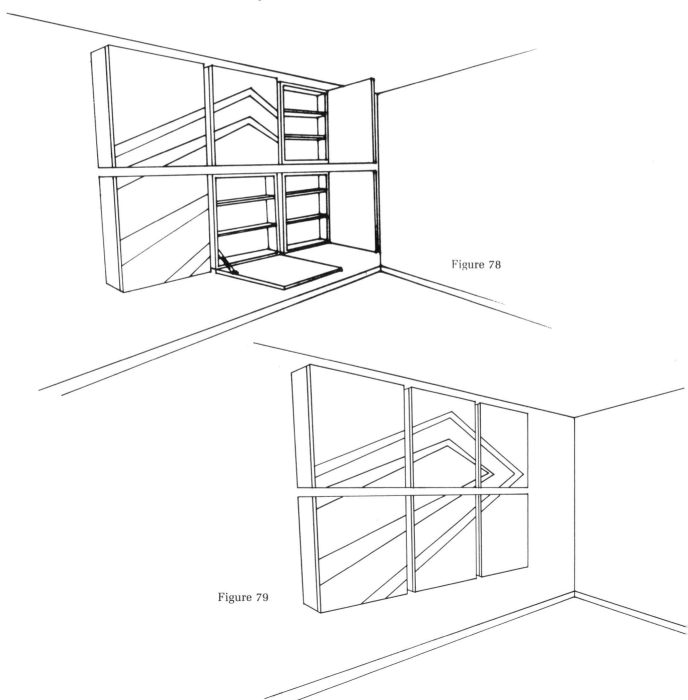

Figure 78

Figure 79

virtue of being quite shallow, taking even less of valuable living space. They are simple boxes with piano-hinged doors and adjustable shelves. Hinged at the bottom and supported by a lid support (the Sears catalog calls it a "fall" support), the door can serve as a writing or bar surface. (See Figure 78.)

In a whimsical moment, these pieces were designed to combine into a bit of supergraphics. There's no reason why you shouldn't do something similar, but you must be able to cut perfect edges to do a satisfactory job. With the use of two or more colors — or even one vivid color — wall cabinets like these can serve as a focal point in a room as a large piece of art might.

# Chapter Six
# BEDS

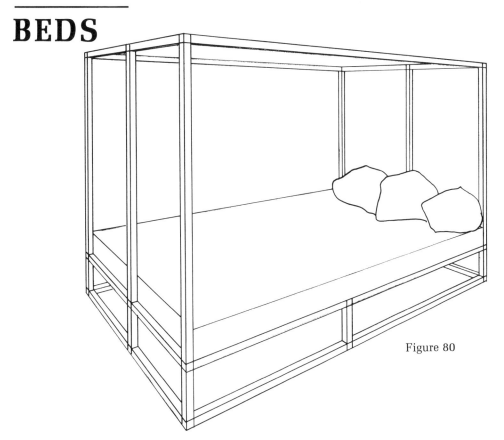

Figure 80

It is unfortunate but true that in twentieth-century America the bed has fallen on bad times. By contrast, in Elizabethan England the bed was considered to be the family's most prized possession. William Shakespeare bequeathed "unto my wife my second best bed." The best bed, in those days, was carefully left to an heir more likely to keep it in the family.

Louis XIV, as did most French monarchs of the era, regularly held court in his bedchamber, lounging on an immense lavishly gilded and silvered structure truly fit for a king. In fact, the royal bed often was so lavish that actual sleeping was done in a smaller adjacent room.

In Colonial America the great four-posted tester was a treasured family possession, and the nineteenth-century Victorian bedroom was dominated by an ornate brass bedstead.

Today's bedroom, likely as not, is to be found built around a box spring and mattress, on the floor or on tiny hidden legs.

One reason, of course, is cost. If dollars are a consideration when the bedroom is being furnished, the bedstead is the easiest piece to eliminate for the moment, allowing purchase of something more vital. But equally important is the fact that the understated look that many persons are trying to achieve in their homes simply is not often available commercially except in high-cost designer pieces.

Each of the pieces to follow does achieve the understated look while still being an attractive piece of furniture, not just a hidden form over which to drape a spread.

The basic bed is a quite simple structure, simply a frame to support and partially enclose a foam mattress. It can be of substantial proportions or show a quite thin profile. It can rest on a visible base, seem to float on a hidden base, or move around on casters for cleansing ease. It can contain most of the height of the mattress or expose most of it, giving the illusion of a much deeper mattress. Whatever its configuration, it is built of $\frac{3}{4}''$ plywood with a $\frac{1}{4}''$ plywood mattress support. It can be integrated with a headboard (Figure 81) or used by itself.

The dimensions of the bed frame as well as your construction methods will depend on the mattress type and size you choose. A latex foam rubber mattress requires no box spring and rests directly on the mattress support. A first-quality foam

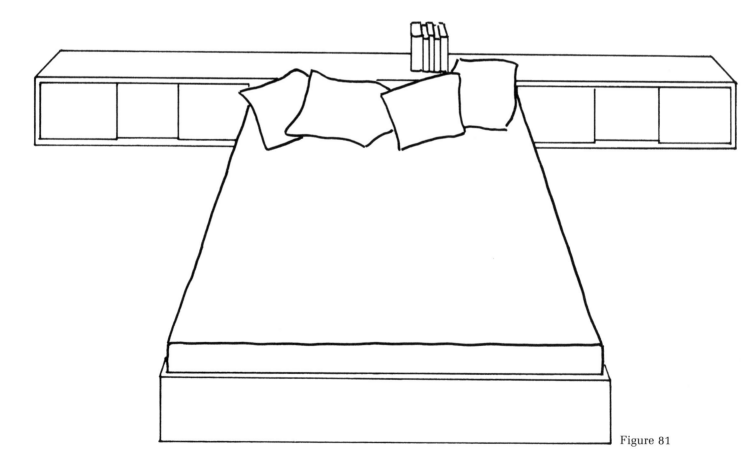

Figure 81

rubber mattress is generally $5\frac{1}{2}''$ thick and comes in a variety of lengths and widths. It is esthetically suited for this type of furniture because it is smooth and flat and makes up with sharp corners.

A conventional innerspring mattress and box spring can also be used if you prefer, but they will somewhat limit your flexibility of design. A typical combination is approximately 14″ thick, so anything built to conceal it would be pretty massive.

The following are standard mattress sizes. You may have to shop around a bit for some of the less common sizes, but they are all available from one source or another.

| | |
|---|---|
| Twin | $39'' \times 75''$ |
| Double | $54'' \times 75''$ |
| Queen | $60'' \times 80''$ |
| King | $78'' \times 80''$ |
| California King | $72'' \times 84''$ |
| Extra-Long King | $78'' \times 84''$ |
| Extra-Long Twin | $39'' \times 80''$ |
| Extra-Long Double | $54'' \times 80''$ |

Depending on the demands of your local climate and your own preferences, you will want to leave up to an inch of clearance between the mattress and frame sides to accommodate the sheets, blankets, and bedspread. Measure the thickness of the bedclothes on your current bed to determine the amount of clearance you'll need.

The bed illustrated (Figure 81) accommodates a queen-sized mattress, so the dimensions here will be based on that size. Your own dimensions will vary depending on your choice of mattress.

## THE BASIC BED

Construction of the basic bed begins with the assembly of the frame. Assuming a bedclothes clearance of 1″ on each side and 1″ at the *foot only*, the bed sides are cut 8″ wide by $82\frac{1}{2}''$ long. The ends are cut 8″ wide by 62″ long and are fitted between the sides for assembly as shown in Figure 82.

Although most of the furniture in this book can be assembled with finishing nails, the stresses and strains on a bed call for assembly with $1\frac{1}{2}''$ No. 8 flathead screws, three at each corner. These relatively large screws are easier to seat if you drill the pilot hole with a Screwmate from your hardware store.

After assembly of the four sides the slats are added. The slats are the same length as the frame ends, 62″, but their height will vary with the amount of mattress you want to expose. The bed shown conceals $1\frac{1}{2}''$ of mattress and, allowing $\frac{1}{4}''$ for the plywood mattress support, has slats $6\frac{1}{4}''$ high.

Beginning at each end of the frame, install a slat against the frame end, then every 12″ toward the middle. The number of slats and spacing at the center will depend

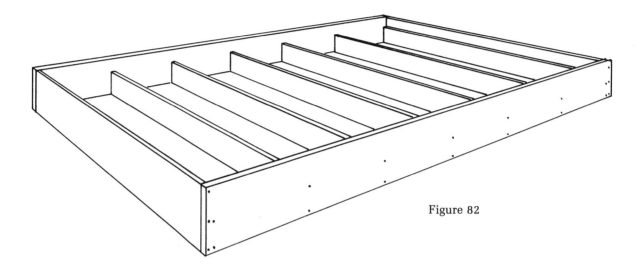

Figure 82

on the bed size, but keep your center spacing 12″ or under. The slats are installed with
$1\frac{1}{4}$″ No. 8 screws, two at each end. They are shown in Figure 82.

If the mattress is more than 48″ wide, the plywood mattress support (see Figure
83) will have to be pieced together from two or more pieces of $\frac{1}{4}$″ material. It doesn't
really make any difference how many pieces as long as all short-dimension joints—
along the slats—fall on the slats so they can be securely nailed. Joints that fall across the
slats needn't be nailed. Be sure, however, to sand the edges of the $\frac{1}{4}$″ plywood so that
no splinters or rough edges can damage the mattress or you.

The bed frame is now ready for mounting on either a platform or casters. A platform is constructed like the platform for the sofa in Figure 32 (page 51) and secured to
the frame with small angle irons.

If the platform is to be visible and obvious, it can be laminated in matching or
contrasting colors. Inset the platform at least 4 inches but not more than 10 inches,
because any deeper inset might cause the bed to tip easily.

If you want the bed to float over a less-obvious platform, inset the platform 10
inches and either laminate it with black plastic or paint it black. Another method of
floating a sofa is to install carpeting that seems to continue up the platform frame.
Just add leftover carpeting to the platform, carefully matching any stripes or patterns.

To mount the bed on casters, you will need to add caster platforms between the
second and third slats at each end. They are attached to the frame sides with two screws
at each end and to the slats with screws every 12 inches.

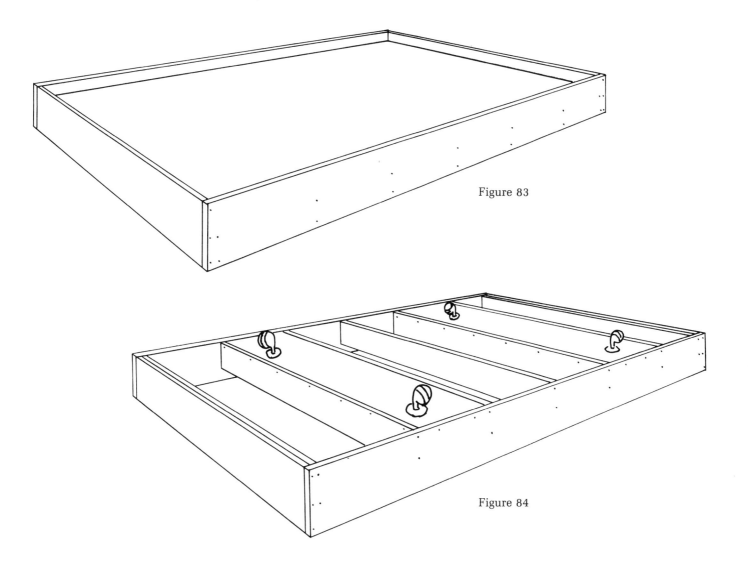

Figure 83

Figure 84

The inner surfaces that surround the mattress are laminated first. In theory, as with some of the sofa seats, this space isn't visible, but it will be at times, particularly at the corners. Cut the plastic to the exact height, in this case $1\frac{1}{2}''$, or just the smallest bit oversize so it can be trimmed with the sander. Next, the outside ends, then the sides, finally the top surfaces. While the top surfaces on at least the smaller beds could be cut from a single piece of plastic, it is more likely that they will be mitered. Remember to cut the strips extra wide as you did for the chest in Figure 66 (page 75), in order to adjust the miter.

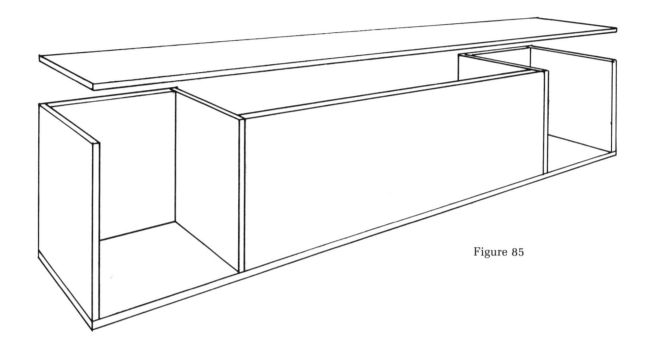

Figure 85

## VARIATIONS

Although this bed can be used by itself, it is perhaps better with an integral headboard. Laminate all inside surfaces of the bookshelf sections—don't forget the top and floor of the sections—and assemble (Figure 85). Laminate first the ends, then the top, then the front. If the front plastic is to be from a single sheet (as it should be on this piece), install the uncut sheet, open up your book sections by making a plunge cut (see Figure 56, page 67), then complete trimming. The book spaces can be left open, with fixed or adjustable shelves (fixed shelves are secured before final lamination). The spaces can also be closed with sliding doors.

The width of the book sections depends on your own needs, but the width of the front panel (between the books) should match exactly the width of the bed itself. It is attached to the bed with three carriage bolts (see Figure 86).

If the bed is to be on casters, the headboard too must be on casters. To reduce the caster cost, put two at the foot of the bed, only one centered at the head of the bed, then two "outriggers" on the headboard. These will stabilize the assembly, with the single caster at the head simply taking the strain off the carriage bolts.

The basic bed can also be supported by runners, inset perhaps 6 inches from each side (Figure 87). The runner ends are laminated first, then the sides. They are secured to the slats by angle irons on the inside. Because of the possible side strain on this kind of base, use at least three 4″ angles on each rail.

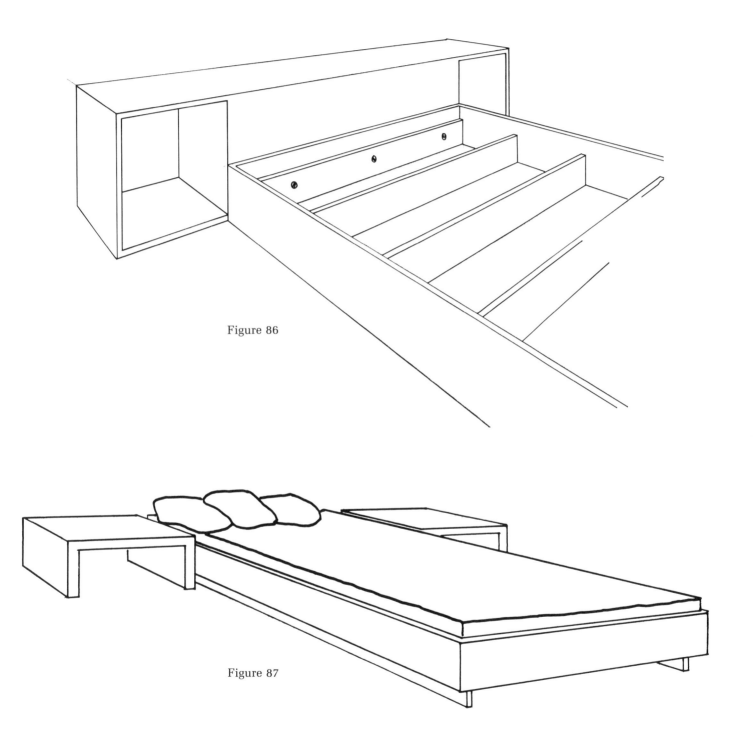

Figure 86

Figure 87

An oversize slab bed serves also as nightstand, TV table, bookcase, and whatever else suits you without adding other pieces of furniture to the room. As shown in Figure 88, it conceals $1\frac{1}{2}''$ of the mattress, exposing the remaining 4 inches. First, assemble and laminate the platform, then attach it to the solid plywood panels with sixpenny nails. The two courses of buildup are then nailed to the solid panel. The hollow section of the first course of spacers (Figure 89) reduces weight a bit but isn't necessary. When the structure is complete, laminate first the inside of the mattress section, then the four outside edges, then the top surface.

I have a notion that at some point in his life every child desperately wants a

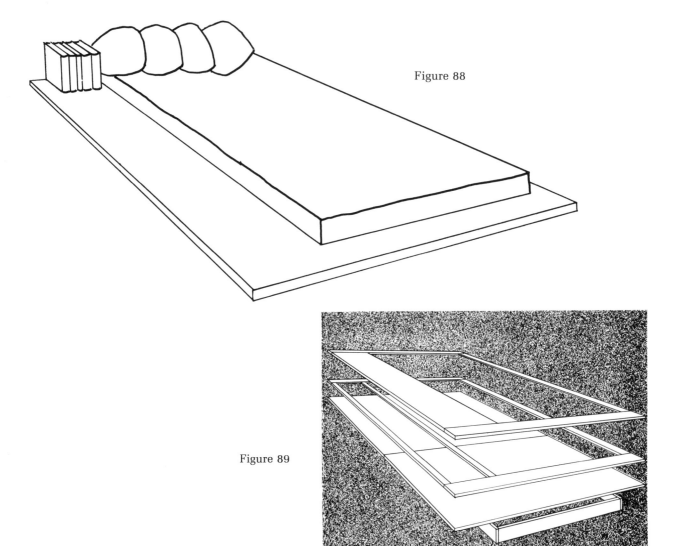

Figure 88

Figure 89

bunk bed. It represents, I suppose, some aspects of adventure, camping out, climbing, living by one's wits. And why not? Here's a simple one.

It consists simply of the head- and footboards, side panels, slat structure, and mattress supports. As shown in Figure 90 the head and foot of each bunk are separate, so the beds can also be used as twins. And the bed must come apart, too, because in not one house out of a hundred could it be moved from workroom to bedroom if it didn't come apart. If that's not a problem, build it in one piece. The unseamed end panels look a little nicer.

Laminate all inside surfaces before assembly. Also before assembly, laminate the

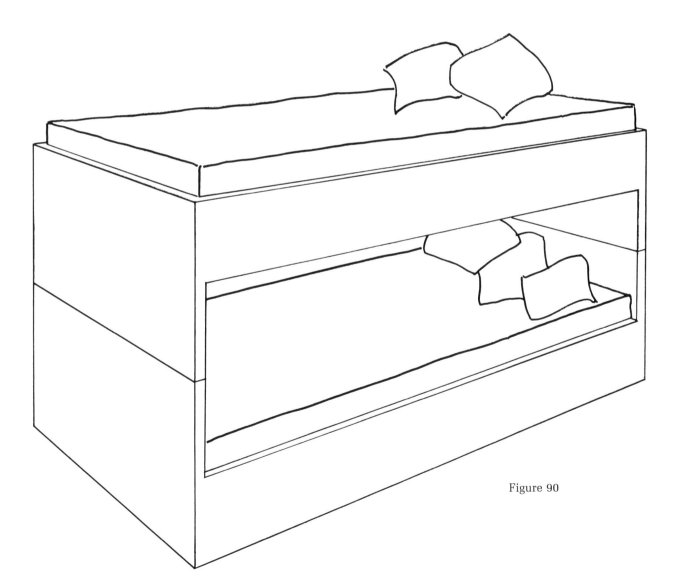

Figure 90

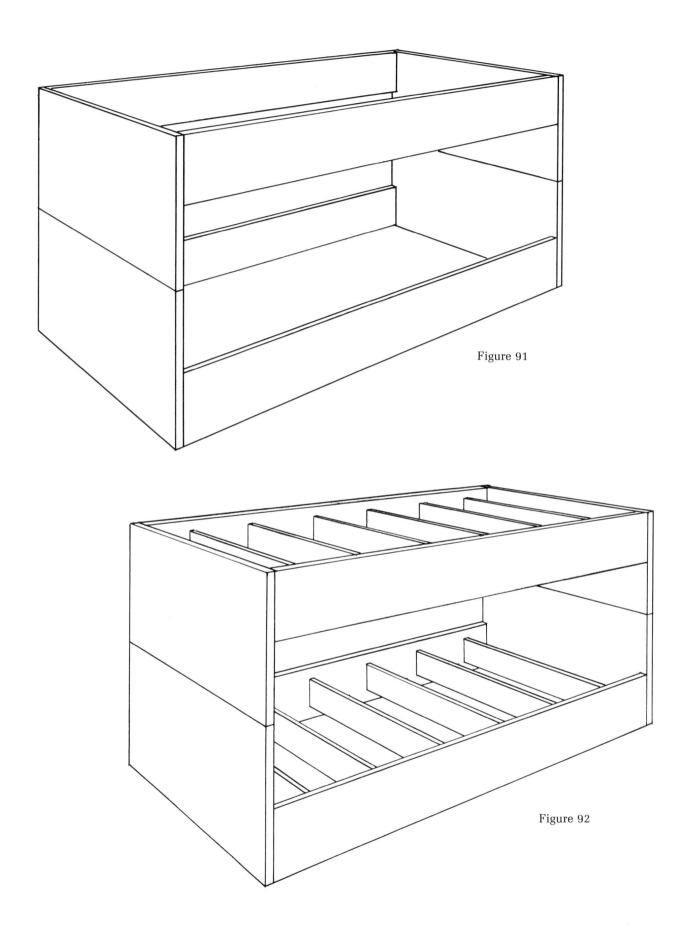

Figure 91

Figure 92

lower edges of the upper side-panels and the upper edges of the lower side-panels. Then assemble the side panels to the heads and feet (Figure 91) with 2″ No. 10 flathead screws.

The upper and lower bunks are held in alignment with 2″ aluminum dowels, cut with a hacksaw from aluminum rod available at your hardware store.

Arrange the side and slat dimensions (see Figure 92) so that the lower bunk can be reversed and used beside the upper one as a twin. As shown (Figure 93), the bunk has 10″ side panels and conceals $1\frac{1}{2}$″ of the mattress. This all yields a $6\frac{1}{2}$″ slat, centered on the side panels, with a $\frac{1}{4}$″ mattress support on each side. The upper section won't be reversed, so it doesn't really need the second mattress support, but it might look a little nicer to the occupant of the lower bunk if you added it. Painted or laminated in white, the support could provide a little better light in the lower bunk.

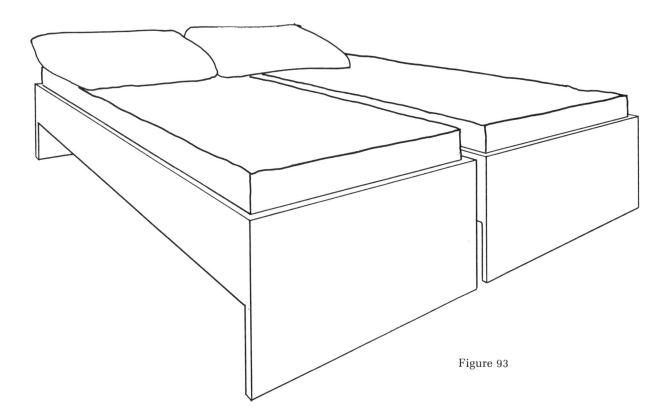

Figure 93

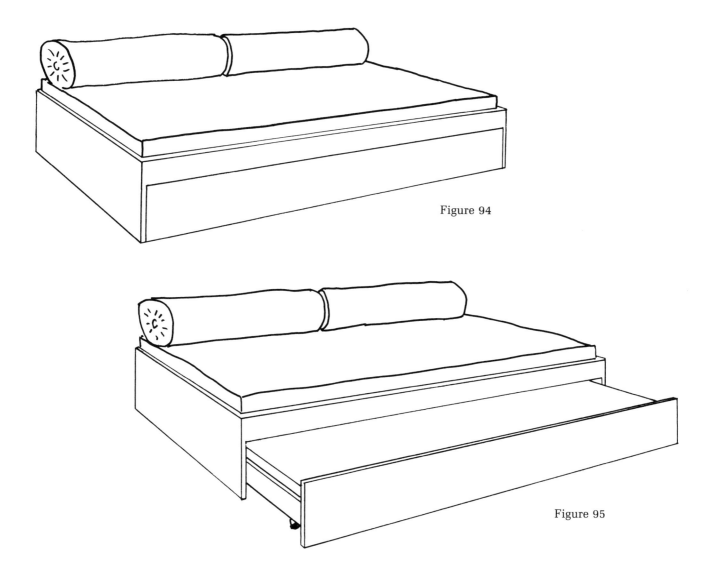

Figure 94

Figure 95

If space is a problem, another solution is a trundle bed. The one in Figure 94 is in two sections. The outer section is built like a section of the bunk bed—with a major exception: Instead of using slats and a $\frac{1}{4}''$ mattress-support, the upper bed uses a $\frac{3}{4}''$ mattress-support resting on cleats like the sofa seats. (Slats have no particular virtue on the earlier beds except that they are the easiest way to support loads more than 4' wide. Any bed under 4' in width should use a $\frac{3}{4}''$ support on cleats.)

Laminate the inner sides of the ends, assemble the sides to the ends as you did with the bunks, attach the cleats, then mount the mattress support. Now laminate the inner side of the mattress well (the ends are already covered with plastic), laminate the ends, then the sides, and finally the mitered top surface.

The lower part—or the actual "trundle"—is simply a box holding the mattress, with a front very much like a drawer front (see Figure 95). To reduce over-all dimensions the lower mattress will have to be shorter than the upper, and if the bed is just for an occasional overnight six-year-old, should be a little thinner.

The "drawer front" is attached to the box with No. 8 screws from the inside. For smooth operation, the trundle should roll on *nonswivel* casters and be guided at each end by two ball-bearing casters. (If these aren't familiar to you, just ask to see them at your hardware store. Their function will be immediately obvious.)

The bed shown at the beginning of this section (Figure 80) is just one of many fanciful designs that can result with the $1\frac{1}{2}''$ metal system. It is all metal with the exception of the plywood mattress supports resting on flanged tubing (see Figure 96).

Figure 96

# Chapter Seven

# TABLES AND SUCH

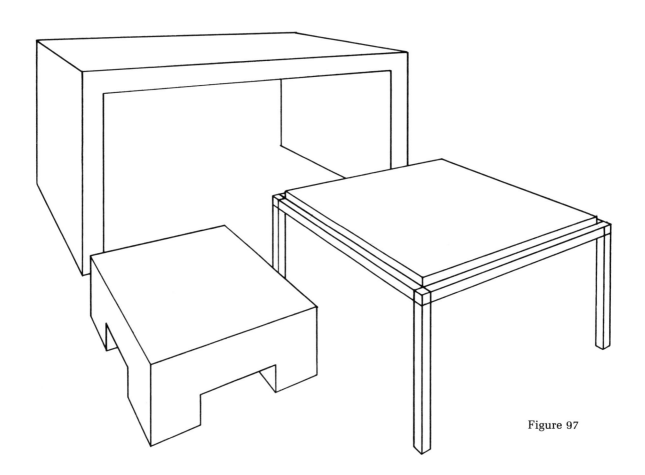

Figure 97

Happiness is having a table wherever and whenever you want it!

Did you ever realize that most homes have a table shortage? You'll find a dining table, surely, and a breakfast table if there's room for it, and few living rooms lack a cocktail table and lamp tables at the most critical spots.

But how about a bedside table for each of your children, or for yourself, for that matter? Is there a cigarette table handy for each of your guests when you're all in the living room or family room? Could Dad carve the turkey a little more elegantly if he had a sideboard nearby? How about a small table in the entrance foyer for mail or packages?

You didn't know what critical shape your table wardrobe was in, did you?

The designs that follow, in most cases, can be built in any size, from tiny snack table to dining table. In some cases the size will affect the construction.

## THE UBIQUITOUS PARSONS TABLE

The Parsons table, probably better than any other piece of furniture, characterizes today's furniture design—functional, utterly simple, yet elegant and obviously a classic design statement. (See Figure 98.) Yet curiously enough, the history of this design isn't completely clear, and there's even a mild controversy about what a Parsons table really is.

First of all, it has nothing to do with a parson, although advertising designers don't seem to be aware of this. Most authorities attribute the design to Jean Michel

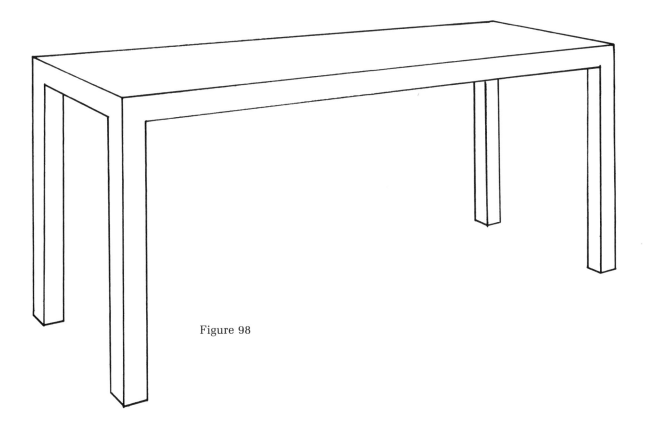

Figure 98

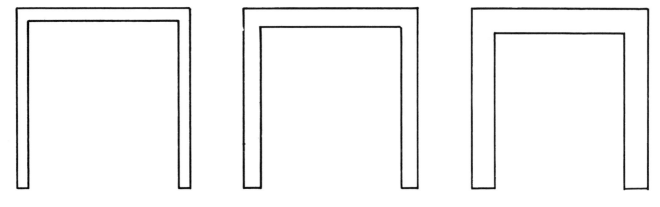

Figure 99

Franck and Joseph Platt, who developed it independently. All agree that it was named for New York's Parsons School of Design.

Some insist that the leg and skirt widths be identical, others that the skirt be a tad wider because it looks smaller to the eye if the dimensions are the same. Some even claim that the legs must be $2\frac{1}{4}''$ and the skirt $2\frac{3}{4}''$. Which, if any, is really correct is academic, although the apron should indeed be a bit larger if it is to look the same as the vertical legs. Just another optical illusion. Increase the dimension about 10 per cent.

A small variation in the dimensions of the legs and skirt will give the finished table a wide variety of weights and "looks." (See Figure 99.) A 30″ game table with 2″ legs and skirt is quite a different table from one with 3″ or 4″ legs and skirt. Neither is preferable. The table should be scaled to your taste and your other furniture.

Construction of all but the smallest Parsons tables is the same as construction of the cube but with an added step. After the profiles are cut, the five components are assembled with sixpenny finishing nails (see Figure 100). The final step is to add the leg backs to each leg (Figure 101). Although the table is quite strong at this point, leg strength is increased a good bit by putting a $1\frac{1}{2}''$ No. 8 flathead screw through the top of the table into each of the eight leg-back components.

Laminate the leg backs first. Because there is no room for machine-trimming where the leg meets the skirt, leave only the slightest margin and remove it with the sander. In most cases, there is room for a laminate trimmer at the back corner of the

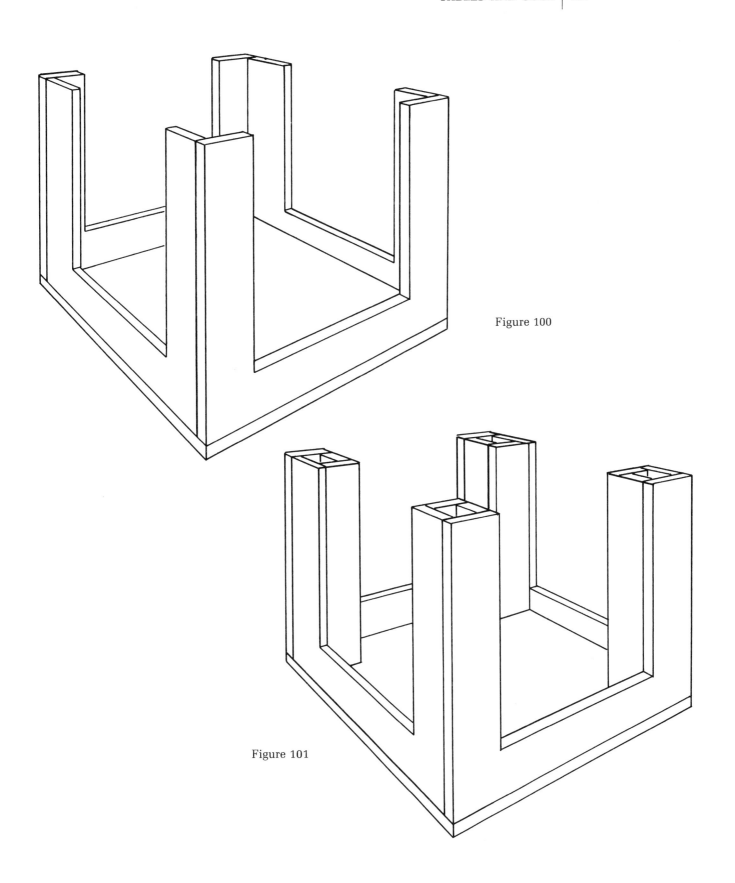

Figure 100

Figure 101

leg but not a conventional router. (See Figure 102.) In this case cut the plastic just a tad oversize, locate the back corners so they need no trimming or sanding at all, and remove the front margin with a sander.

The plastic needn't extend up the leg under the skirt because it isn't visible unless you have very small, critical children.

When the leg backs are complete, finish the lamination as you did with the cube.

The smaller snack or cigarette tables which can be scattered about the room are

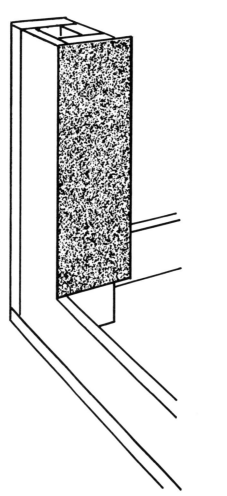

Figure 102

constructed a bit differently. Cut the full-size profile in two sides, attach to the table-top, then complete the buildup until all legs and skirt are uniform (Figure 105). Notice that in this case the tabletop doesn't sit *atop* the sides but *between* them (Figure 104). So, in the case of a 16″ table, the two sides are 16″ by 16″ and the top is 16″ by 14½″ The legs are 2″, a combination of the ¾″ side and a ¾″ and a ½″ spacer. The same is true of the skirt.

Scaling up the leg and skirt size as your tables get larger is a matter of taste, but

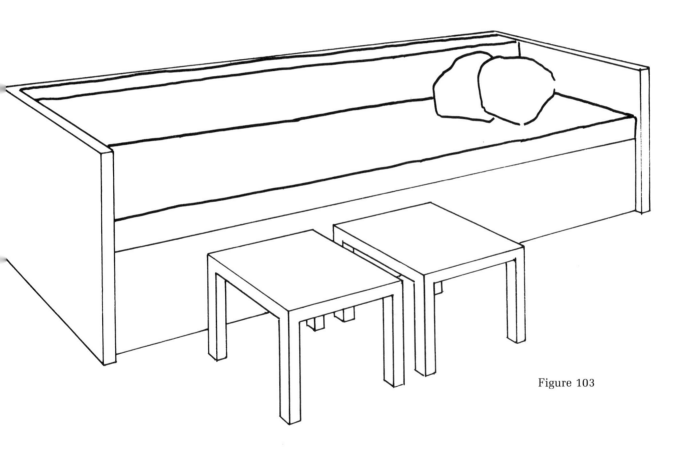

Figure 103

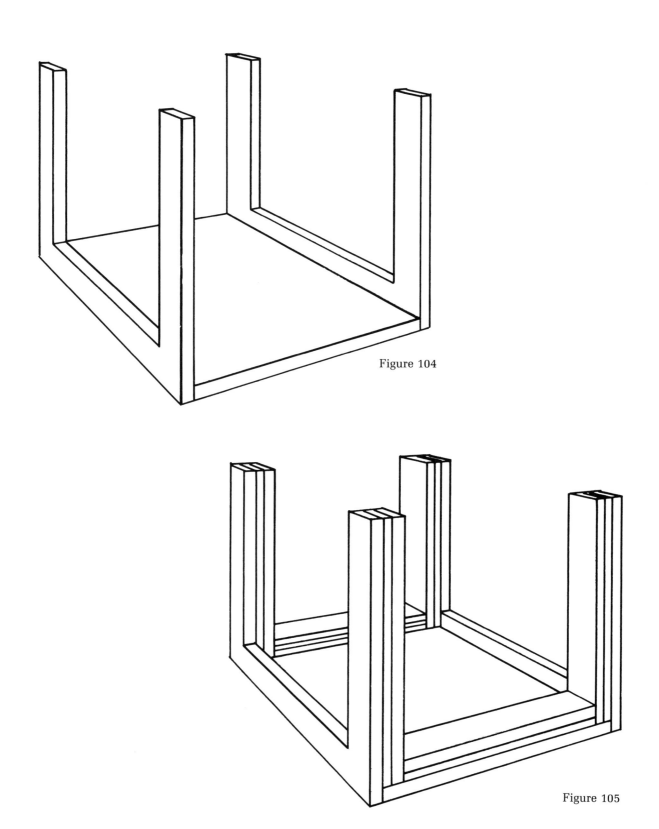

Figure 104

Figure 105

the following can serve as guides. The little 16″ tables should have legs of perhaps $1\frac{1}{2}″$ or 2″. A cocktail table might have legs in the 2″-to-$2\frac{1}{2}″$ range, a game table anywhere from 2″ to 4″ or so. A full-size dining table, perhaps 30″ × 72″, or even 96″, might indeed look splendid in a small-scale dimension but would be more than a little bouncy. Plan the legs for your full-size tables at at least 3″ and preferably 4″ or so. Before lamination on any large table put a typical load on it. If it is bouncy or shows any visible sag, it must have more support. Start with a single center brace (see Figure 106). The brace is attached with $1\frac{1}{2}″$ screws through the top and the ends. If the table still isn't stable, put additional braces behind the two lengthwise skirts.

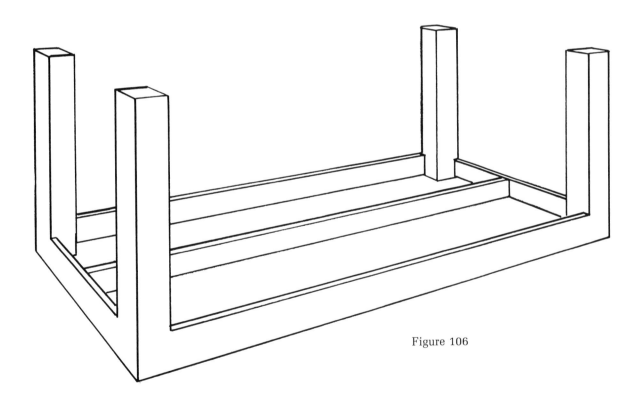

Figure 106

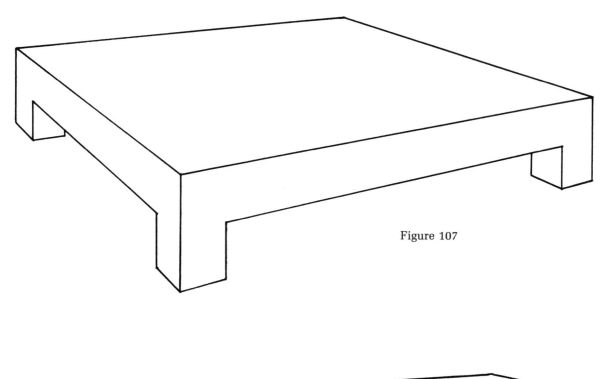

Figure 107

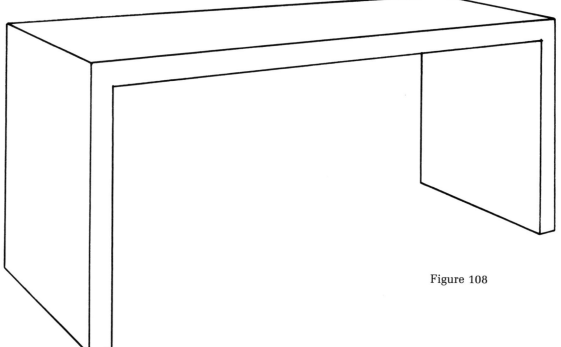

Figure 108

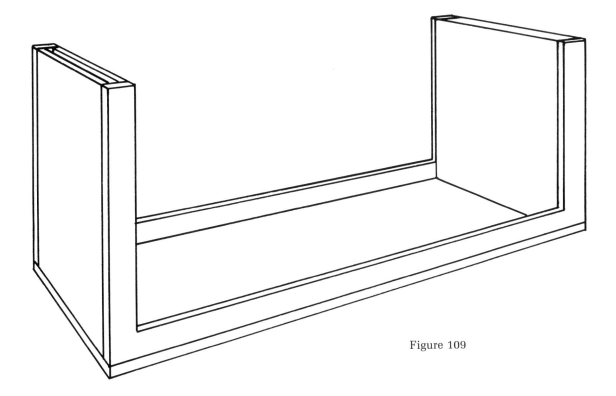

Figure 109

Now that you've read all the rules for leg dimension, feel free to break them. (See Figure 107.)

A popular variation on the Parsons table is the U table (Figure 108), simply a Parsons table with the ends closed. Over the range of sizes the same-leg-and-skirt-dimension suggestions apply. You might hesitate to use this as a dining table, however, because there is no "head of the table."

The side profiles are cut like the Parsons profiles and, again, sit under the table-top. The inner and outer legs are added, and the table is ready for lamination (Figure 109).

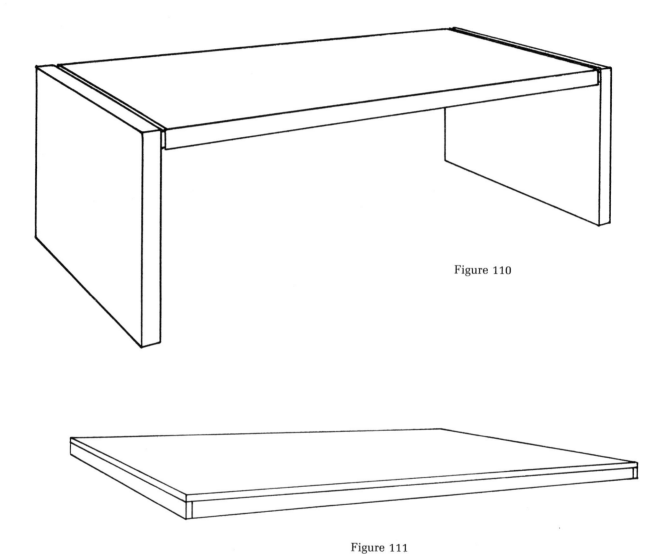

Figure 110

Figure 111

A variation on the U separates the legs from the tabletop with small spacers (Figure 110). It begins with the top, with a $2\frac{1}{4}''$ skirt on all four sides, yielding a 3″ top (Figure 111). This piece is completely laminated.

Because the legs bolt directly to the end skirt sections and have a lot of leverage, the top assembly must be quite strong. Assemble it with $1\frac{1}{2}''$ screws and reinforce each corner on the inside with a 4″ angle iron.

Apply the plastic to the inner surface of the inner leg panel. The inner leg panel

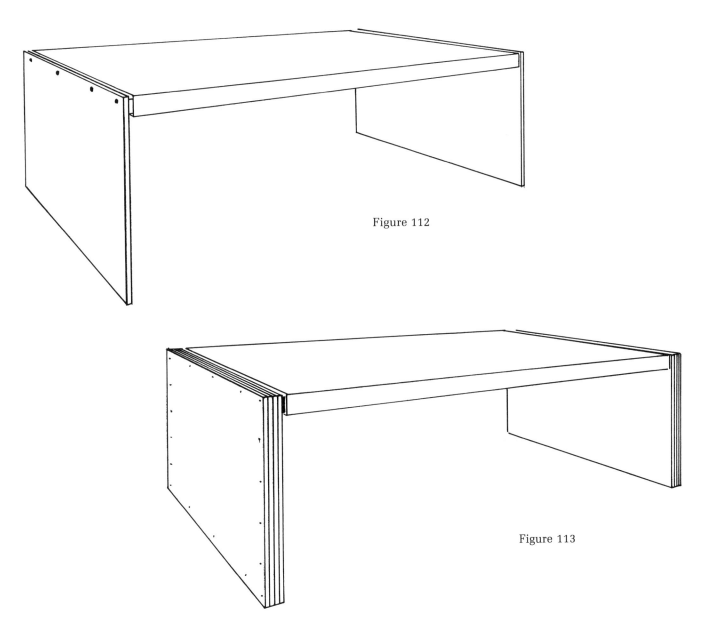

Figure 112

Figure 113

is bolted to the top assembly, separated by a $\frac{1}{4}''$ spacer inset $\frac{1}{4}''$ on all four sides (Figure 112). The spacer can be $\frac{1}{4}''$ hardboard with the edges painted black, or hardboard or plywood with the edges laminated. To laminate the edges follow the procedures for laminating the thin sliding doors on page 68.

When the bolts are installed, complete the buildup to the desired thickness, in this case 3″. (See Figure 113.)

When the plastic is applied to this 3″ leg edge, it can be machine-trimmed and sanded on the outer corner, but there is no machine room on the inner corner. As you did for the Parsons table legs, apply the plastic so that it requires no trimming. (See Figure 102.)

Complete the table by laminating the outer leg panels.

It's not very useful in dining-table size, because there's no place to put your feet, but an inverted U is quite useful as a cocktail table. It is also useful as a hall table or a sideboard.

Build it as the previous U was constructed, but cap off the ends, in this case tops, of the legs and make the top the bottom, so to speak (Figure 114).

The lamination sequence changes a good deal. First laminate the large floor surface, then the inner legs. There is no room for machine-trimming, so cut the plastic components accurately and trim with the sander on the outer edges. Next laminate the outer legs, then the long profiles, finally the two tops.

The tabletop might be simply a $\frac{3}{4}''$ panel completely laminated (top and bottom for balance, remember?), but it's more effective to use a clear top. Good-quality glass, not window glass, or Plexiglas makes a stunning piece.

The thickness of the glass or Plexiglas will depend on the size of the table and

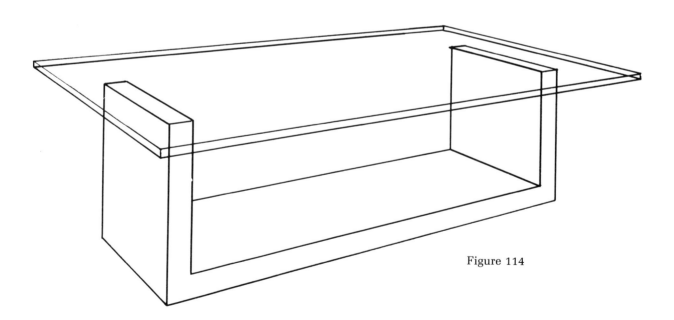

Figure 114

the length of the span. Your glass dealer will make recommendations. Any large span will require $\frac{1}{2}''$ Plexiglas, but a smaller piece gets by nicely with $\frac{1}{4}''$ material. When using Plexiglas, cut it so that it extends outward from the supports a good deal, providing balance and helping to eliminate sag between the supports. And turn the Plexiglas over once in a while.

The preceding tables can all be constructed of Plexiglas as well as plywood. The Parsons tables in Plexiglas are built like those in plywood with one exception: The tops of the leg-back components are polished and are *not* welded to the tabletop.

The U tables are the same, again with the inner leg top not welded to the tabletop.

The modified U, with the inset spacers, requires that the legs be simply Plexiglas boxes rather than built-up sections as with plywood. Since the bolts will be visible through the plastic, use something decorative. Stainless steel or bronze marine hardware is ideal, or you can have common hardware plated at little cost. Look in the Yellow Pages under "Electroplaters."

The vivid clear colors of the laminate and the sparkle of Plexiglas combine nicely. This little cocktail table in Figure 115 has a top built up to $1\frac{1}{2}''$, but any dimen-

Figure 115

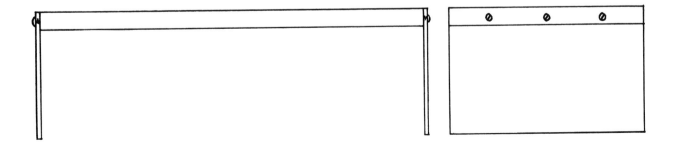

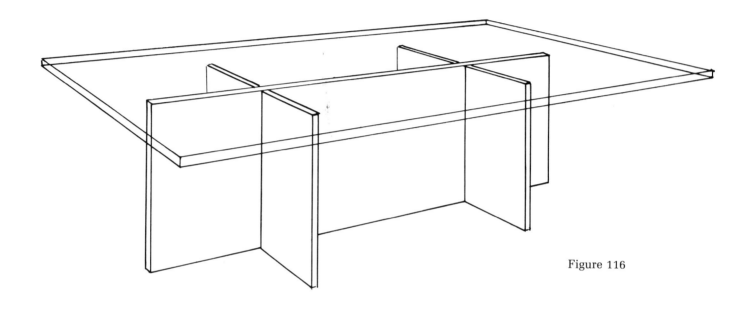

Figure 116

sion can be used. It can, of course, be built as a little square piece to scatter around the room for ashtrays and snacks. For a cocktail or snack table the Plexiglas ends can be $\frac{1}{4}''$ material. A larger version will require $\frac{1}{2}''$ Plexiglas. Polish all four edges of the Plexiglas legs and attach them to the completely laminated top with decorative screws.

The egg-crate table—in the dim past, egg crates were slotted together—can be used in a wide range of sizes, from smallest cocktail table to full-size dining table. Its top can be laminated, glass, or Plexiglas. The table itself (see Figure 116) can be made of Plexiglas, laminated plywood, or cabinet-grade birch plywood. In birch, it is at its best finished with a bright-colored transparent stain, giving the wood color while not covering its grain, with the plywood edges left just as they are instead of covered.

The trick is sawing the slots accurately. Make the long saw cuts for the slots (Figure 117), then finish cutting the slot with a chisel. If the table is being done in birch plywood or Plexiglas, the slot is exactly the width of the material thickness. If it is in laminated plywood, you must also allow for two $\frac{1}{16}''$ plastic sheets. Also, allow just the width of a pencil line for the adhesive.

Laminate and trim all the edges first, then the sides. The plastic can be trimmed around the slot only with a router. There isn't sufficient clearance for the mechanism of the laminate trimmer or the hand trimmer. If you don't have a router, carefully lay out the slots in the plastic before lamination, leaving very small margins on the plastic. Laminate carefully, then finish by filing the slots clean with a fine file. Don't tackle this method unless you have a saintly amount of patience.

The metal system is ideal for tables large and small. It's strong, lightweight, and easily cleaned and happily takes the jolts and knocks that occasional tables invariably get.

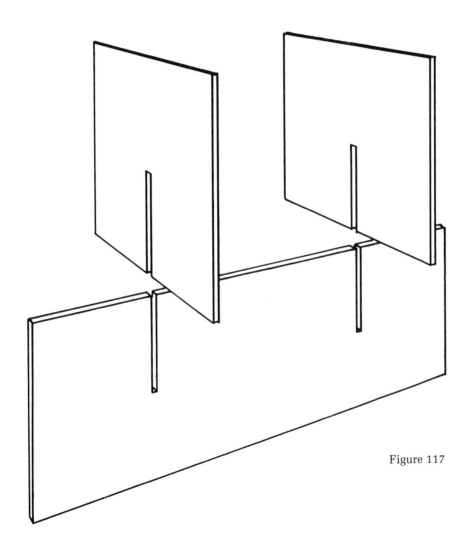

Figure 117

This cocktail table (Figure 118) is a $\frac{3}{4}''$ top with a $\frac{3}{4}''$ skirt, completely laminated. The long horizontal sections of $\frac{3}{4}''$ tubing are attached with wood screws from the inside of the tabletop. They needn't be attached by the elaborate method used for the sofa in Figures 46, 47, and 48 (pages 59 and 60).

The leg sections are then attached.

The little Parsons-like table in Figure 119 is built of the $1\frac{1}{2}''$ system and has a butcher-block top. The long, unsupported legs would seem to be unstable and begin to wobble, but this table has been rolling around my kitchen for a year or so and is as stable as the day it was built. The legs are of plain tubing; the horizontal pieces are flanged on the inside to support the top. Because the metal system doesn't include a component for attaching casters, you'll have to close the ends of the tubing with wood. Cut wedges of wood, drive them into the legs as far as possible, then cut off the wedges flush with the metal. The platform casters screw directly to this plug.

A similar structure in cocktail-table proportions (Figure 120) could also be topped with butcher block or with a laminated panel. This one, however, is topped with a smoky Plexiglas box containing a Mirrorlite mirror. The box is just large enough to contain and protect the mirror's surface.

Mirrorlite, an unbreakable, superior-quality mirror, is used because of its safety

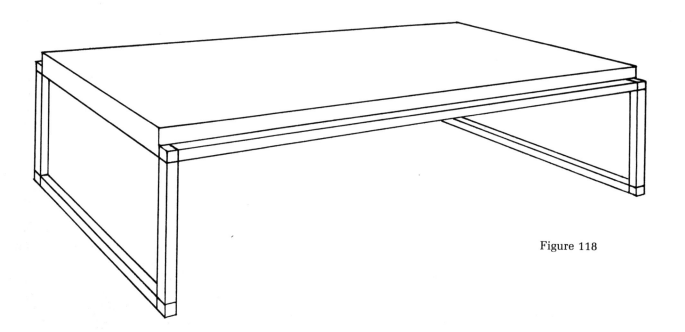

Figure 118

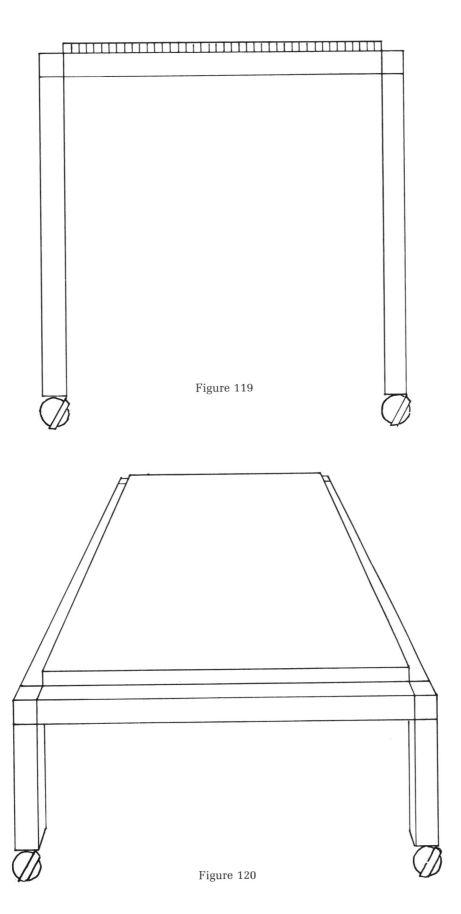

Figure 119

Figure 120

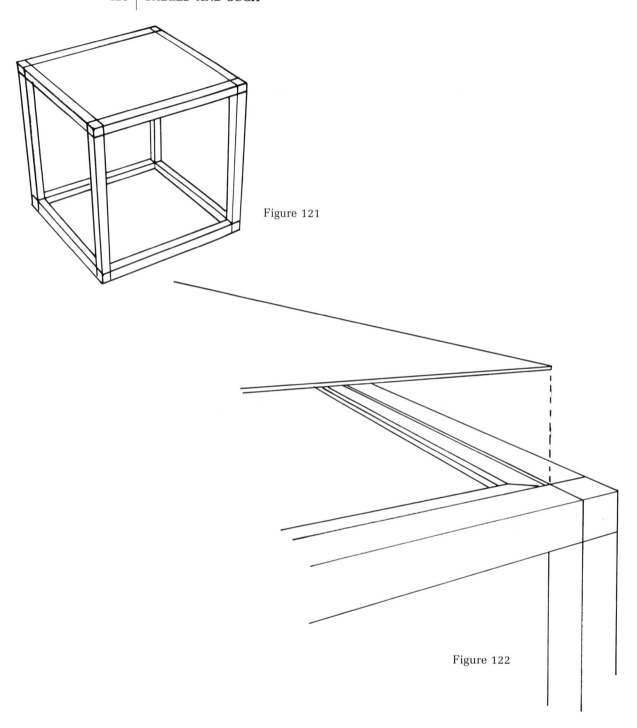

Figure 121

Figure 122

and light weight. It can't be used directly as a table surface, though, because it consists of silvered polyester film stretched over a frame very much as an artist's canvas is stretched.

The little $\frac{3}{4}''$ metal system can be fashioned into a variety of casual, lightweight tables. The series of cubes here demonstrates top configurations appropriate for tables for any purpose.

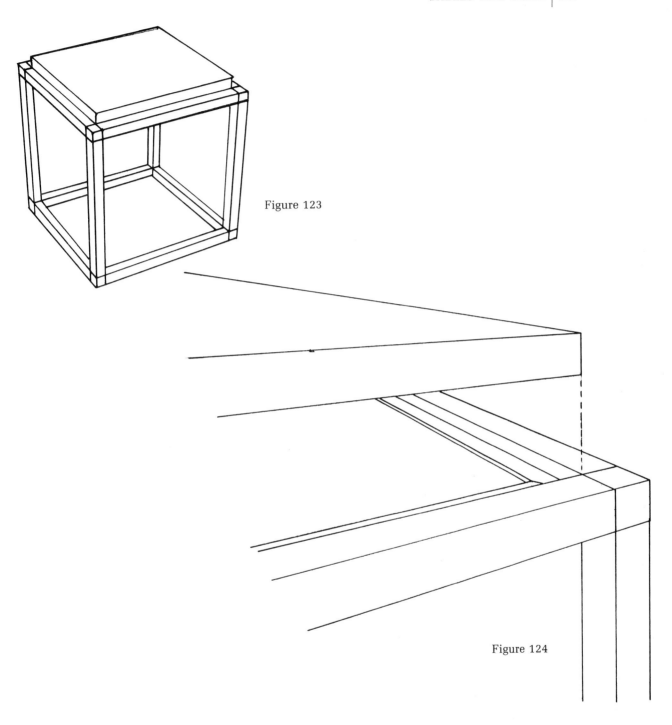

Figure 123

Figure 124

A flush-top table (Figures 121 and 122) consists of an unmounted panel of plastic resting on flanges. The plastic is stiffened and made heavy enough to stay in place by gluing a square of plywood, small enough to clear the flange, to the underside of the panel.

Flanges also support the laminated $\frac{3}{4}''$ top in Figures 123 and 124. The top could also be butcher block, perhaps marble, or heavy glass.

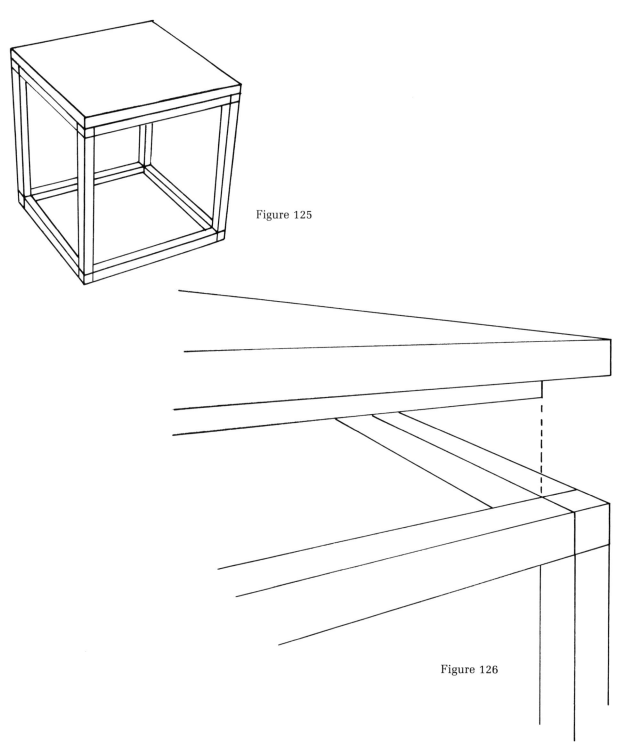

Figure 125

Figure 126

The flush top in Figures 125 and 126 is a piece of $\frac{3}{4}''$ plywood, laminated, and held securely in place with a panel underneath, fitting within the plain tubing. Remember to cut the plywood $\frac{1}{8}''$ smaller than the dimensions of the metal cube, allowance for the plastic thickness.

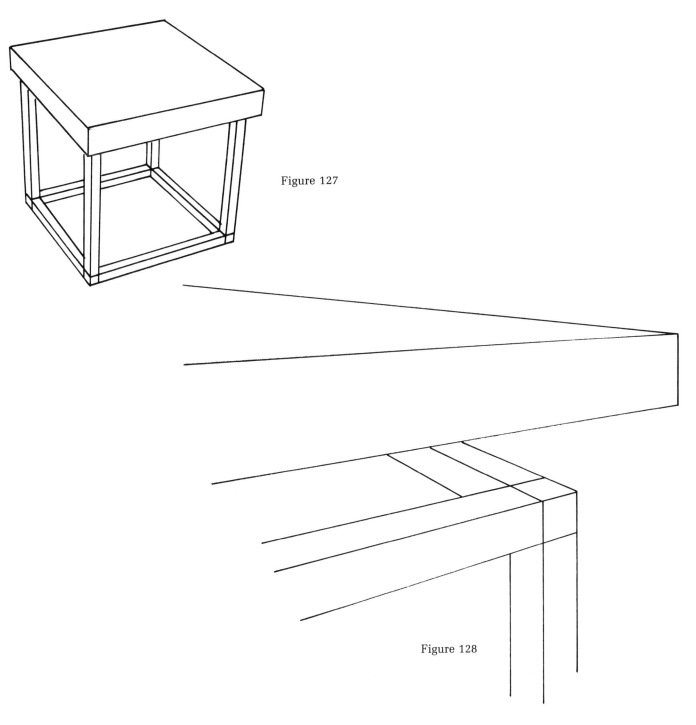

Figure 127

Figure 128

The table in Figures 127 and 128 is simply a metal cube with a cap top. The top is $\frac{3}{4}''$ thick with a $\frac{3}{4}''$ skirt on all four sides.

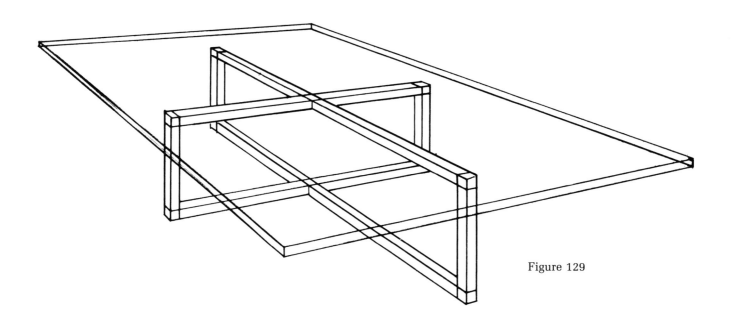

Figure 129

Either the large or the small aluminum system can be developed into any number of fanciful table bases (Figures 129, 130, and 131). The configuration isn't really important as long as contact with the floor is made in four places, reasonably well distributed. Tops of glass, laminate, or Plexiglas are all appropriate.

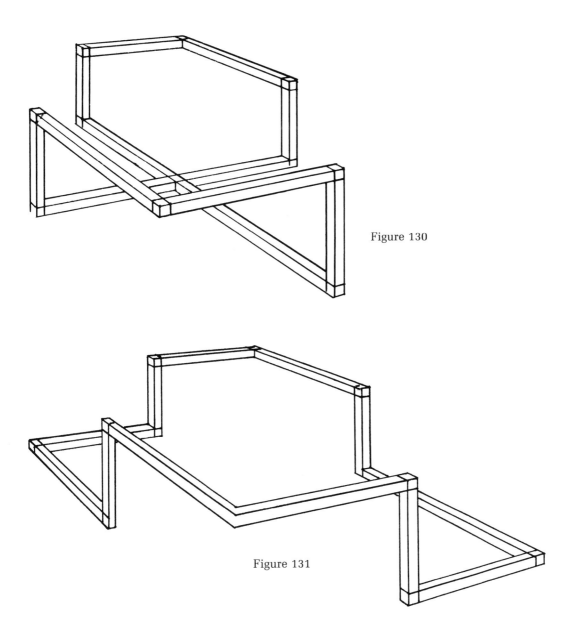

Figure 130

Figure 131

# Buyer's Guide

*For aluminum systems:*
    AMCO Engineering Co.
    7333 W. Ainslie St.
    Chicago, Ill. 60656
    Request catalogs 203 and 208


*For hand laminating tools:*
    Beno J. Gundlach Co.
    Dept. WS, Box 544
    Belleville, Ill. 62222


*For information on Plexiglas:*
    Rohm & Haas˙
    Philadelphia, Pa. 19105


*For Rucaire poromeric fabric:*
    Hooker Chemical Corporation
    295 Fifth Avenue
    New York, N. Y. 10016


*For Mirrorlite:*
    Kamar Products, Inc.
    2 South Buckhout Street
    Irvington-on-Hudson, N. Y. 10533

# Index